MW01600776

Advance Praise for *Without Warning*

"Johnson transforms 'silence' into a 'sonic boom' of breakthroughs! It's relevant and on target. Get it on your bookshelf, on your nightstand, or in your briefcase. Now!"

—Jeff Blackman, speaker and best selling author: *Stop Whining! Start Selling!* and *Peak Your Profits*

"*Without Warning* provides breakthrough insights into the toxic nature of silent problems and imparts bold new concepts around how to solve them. I encourage everyone to read this book, and put its principles to work. I did."

—Joan Skluzacek, founder, IDEA League

"In these uncertain times, silent problems have countless implications. This book imparts amazing insight into how to transform their silence, into energized action."

—Richard Carr, senior advisor and vice chairman of the Board, Vistage International

"Silent problems quietly conquer a company's ability to compete. Rodney Johnson's book addresses a topic that no one is talking about, but desperately needs to be heard. Read this book to discover new strategies and effective solutions to help your business achieve greater success. You will never think of business the same way again!"

—Sarah L. Sladek, Limelight Generations

without WARNING

Breakthrough strategies for solving the
silent problems taking aim at your organization

RODNEY N. JOHNSON

ADAMS
BUSINESS &
PROFESSIONAL
A division of Beaver's Pond Press

ISBN 10: 1-59298-274-3
ISBN 13: 978-1-59298-274-5

Library of Congress Catalog Number: 2009922832

Printed in the United States of America

First Printing: 2009

13 12 11 10 09   5 4 3 2 1

Cover and interior design by James Monroe Design, LLC.

Adam's Business & Professional
7104 Ohms Lane, Suite 101
Edina, MN 55439–2129
952-829-8818
www.BeaversPondPress.com

To order, visit www.BookHouseFulfillment.com
or call 1-800-901-3480. Reseller discounts available.

To my son Justin
Inspiration, Insight, and Joy

Contents

Introduction

Ahhh ... People ask me questions, lost in confusion.
Well, I tell them there's no problem, only solutions.
Well, they shake their heads and they look at me as if
I've lost my mind.

Watching the Wheels *by John Lennon*

On June 14, 2002, an asteroid the size of a soccer field traveled within 75,000 miles of Earth (a distance much nearer than the moon), traveling at 23,000 miles per hour. Surprisingly, this close encounter with Asteroid 2002MN wasn't detected until three days later. As Steve Maran of the American Astronomical Society said, "It's a good thing it missed the Earth because we never saw it coming." And then he went on to say, "At some level, it behooves us to look out for these things."

In 2008, an asteroid of a different type, yet equally large and dangerous approached the financial district of Manhattan. This asteroid, however, was a direct hit, sending reverberations around the globe. It impaled the likes of Bear Stearns, AIG, Lehman Brothers, Fannie Mae, and Freddie Mac, along with numerous other financial

institutions. The fallout was monumental as many institutions crumbled under their own weight. Some filed for
bankruptcy. Others were hastily sold to other financial
institutions. And still others sought protection from the
U.S. Treasury.

Situations similar to Asteroid 2002MN take place
at every level and in every dimension of an organization.
Some might fall under the umbrella of a natural disaster.
However, most are simply problems. In fact, I've often
wondered why we so often miss problems like asteroids
hurling toward us. Where do they come from, and how
do I avoid them?

Are these occurrences simply a problem waiting to
happen?

No, these are problems that have already happened
or are happening. We just don't see them. A problem
waiting to happen rarely exists. For instance, the 2008
sub-prime financial fallout was simply a problem that
was being ignored and avoided on numerous fronts.
New York University economist Nouriel Roubini had
sounded warnings several years earlier, only to be dismissed and his findings disregarded by other economists.
In 2006, the Office of Federal Housing Enterprise Over-
sight (OFHEO), responsible for monitoring the financial
health of Freddie Mac and Fannie Mae, released a report
revealing a culture of hubris and cover up between 1998
and 2004. Once again, OFHEO and the report were
disregarded, this time by numerous governmental agencies. And even Warren Buffet came to the party describ-
ing financial derivatives as "toxic waste." Yet even with
these warning signs, no corrective action was taken by

the federal agencies entrusted with this responsibility. A September 17, 2008, Knowledge@Wharton article titled, "Eyes on the Wrong Prize: Leadership Lapses That Fueled Wall Street's Fall," states:

> *Alarm bells should have gone off... But in many major industries, problems grow slowly and come to be accepted by members of the industry, only to explode later.*

To refer to incidences similar to these as problems "waiting to happen" simply isn't true. These are problems that many people were conscious of, yet no one addressed. In effect, these were silent problems.

Marshall McLuhan, a famous Canadian philosopher and author, once said,

> *We look at the present through a rearview mirror; we walk backwards into the future.*

Today, silent problems are one of the greatest "rearview mirror" challenges facing every organization, every business, and every public institution. These are the problems that suddenly surface with the corresponding moniker, "I should have seen that one coming" or "I knew a problem existed, yet I didn't realize it had become so big, and tenacious." But more often than not, we ignore, avoid, and shun the signals coming to us through our forward-looking windshield. Instead, we deal with the myriad of issues and problems that are on our desk today.

For over three years, I've had the opportunity to explore and live the silent problem phenomenon. At times, I worked with the problems directly in my work with

CEOs and their organizations. At other times, I studied them from a historical context, trying to identify their nuances and subtle idiosyncrasies. I've examined why they exist and, more importantly, why leaders are inclined to neglect them, even if they're aware of them. I've studied how silent problems can be successfully brought out of the closet and into the light of day for everyone to see. And most important, I've identified sound solutions and created solid processes that you can use to solve silent problems under the most demanding of conditions.

This book is your road map for taking control of the silent problems that reside inside your organization. It's a resource to help leaders and their organizations identify and solve silent problems. For in today's competitive landscape, little trip-ups or even slight miscalculations can have a disproportionate effect on results. I'm convinced that dealing with silent problems is relevant to personal success and critical to the viability and future success of every business, institution, and public entity.

This book will investigate the toxic and virulent nature of silent problems and expose them before they explode. And most important, this book will help you understand the strategy, tactics, and execution to solving the silent problems in your organization.

I

*The problem
with problems*

ONE

The Archetypes

Our lives begin to end the day we become silent upon things that matter.
Martin Luther King Jr.

Childhood books are sacred objects in my library, especially fairy tales from some of the great authors and collectors like Charles Perrault (Cinderella), Jacob and Wilhelm Grimm (Hansel and Gretel), and Hans Christian Anderson (The Emperor's New Clothes). I value these books not because they bring back toasty childhood memories, but because they're filled with fascinating ways to navigate reality and provide guidance to adults.

Despite the distinct and stylistic differences of the various authors, and their contrasting story elements, I'm awestruck by how fairy tales and real life tend to mirror each other. Maria Tatar, author and leading authority on children's literature, states this succinctly: "Fairy tales are up close and personal, telling us about the quest for romance and riches, for power and privilege, and, most important, for a way out of the woods and back to the safety and security of home."

> TODAY, BEING BRIGHT AND TALENTED ISN'T ENOUGH.
>
> ONE MUST ALSO KNOW HOW TO NAVIGATE AND SURVIVE
>
> IN A WORLD GOVERNED BY CONSTANT AND,
>
> AT TIMES, BARBARIC CHANGE.

In my personal journey to find a way out of the woods, I've come to appreciate an equally provocative and less obvious theme. This theme tells the story of leaders and their followers, and that of power versus force—the core underpinnings for most silent problems. Cinderella, Jack and the Beanstalk, and Little Red Riding Hood are but a few of the notable stories that address these competing themes. The main characters experience unexpected and unjust hardships. Yet despite their challenges, they eventually reach a victorious and triumphant ending. Along that journey, the storyteller exposes how followers can become leaders and how power does trump force.

Yes, fairy tales tend to be up close and personal. At times, we too are asked to tackle some of the most difficult and thorny issues of the day. Not run-of-the-mill problems, but rather problems that could represent grave danger. At other times, similar problems might expose one's career, create moral and ethical dilemmas, or place a business in harm's way. Today, being bright and talented isn't enough. One must also know how to navigate and

8

survive in a world governed by constant and, at times, barbaric change. After all, there are hundreds of stories about individuals positioned for greatness who lost their way and sacrificed their self, their career, and, occasionally, their independence. Some of these individuals bear a striking resemblance to fairy tale characters such as a wicked stepmother, a money-thirsty king, or a jealous sibling. Names like Bernie Ebbers (Worldcom), Andy Fastow (Enron), Al Dunlap (Sunbeam Corporation), Bernard Madoff (Madoff Investment Securities), and Dick Fuld (Lehman Brothers) come to mind. And every once in a while, a stranger-than-fiction story emerges, like the tale of a man recognized around the world for being a slayer of great dragons and monsters, but in the end, the sword he used to slay dragons eventually turned inward and impaled him. This would be former New York State Attorney General and Governor of New York, Elliot Spitzer.

There is little doubt that participating in and winning in a world that is connected, mobile, and increasingly transparent can be challenging, creating a multitude of problems for political and business leaders alike, and their organizations. The problems one is expected to solve arrive with risks attached. The potential for failure is real. At times, the opportunity for a happily ever after ending appears remote at best. Yet this is the sandbox where most political and business leaders play, and at times are asked to leave. It's also this same sandbox where many followers find themselves, contemplating whether to follow their leaders in the games they play or to pursue a different path, one they believe can truly make a difference.

In the following pages, I'll show how courageous individuals found themselves ensnared by the silent problems their personal sandbox contained. Problems they weren't prepared to take on, much less solve. Yet despite extreme odds, they won. For every leader that may have become lost, there are equally captivating scenarios and stories that illustrate how individuals and groups exposed silent problems for the world to see and implemented sound solutions. Along their journeys, nuggets of knowledge surfaced, revealing

- how they embedded vitality into their cause and made it come to life

- how they exploited their power, authority, and influence to overturn the existing order

- how they created and embedded change

- how they minimized risk and enhanced their probability for success

- how they found the seed to plant that lifted them up into the clouds, enabling them to defeat a giant and return home triumphant.

This is a book about really tough problems and how to create a winning strategy that will make a difference.

TWO

Three Types of Problems Plus One

*Some problems are so complex that you have
to be highly intelligent and well informed just to be
undecided about them.*

Laurence Peter

Problem n. Any question or matter involving doubt,
uncertainty, or difficulty. n. A question proposed
for solution or discussion.

Problems are our greatest challenge and opportunity, our
greatest strength and weakness, and our greatest chance
for success or failure. Most of the time, problems present a challenge to be pursued and eventually solved. And
if we're successful, we're rewarded with financial incentives, promotions, and public recognition. Yes, the spoils
go to those who can solve problems.

But what should we do with problems that are silent, are inherently risky, or have a low probability for success? Should we avoid, or should we pursue?

If we avoid, do we assume the problem will eventually solve itself or go away given enough time?

If we avoid, do we expect that if the problem doesn't solve itself, at the very least, it won't get any worse?

If we avoid, is it because we're avoiding the conflict the problem might create?

If we're caught in a quandary whether to avoid or solve a problem, do we believe that avoiding it might be the lesser of two evils?

If we avoid, are we proclaiming the problem isn't all that important?

To start this journey, it's important to understand and appreciate the bigger picture of problems and to demystify them.

Simple Problems

The traditional problem-solving approach is linear and is well suited for most problems we encounter in our day-to-day lives. Nancy Roberts, an instructor at the Monterey Naval Post Graduate School, refers to these as "Simple Problems." The "waterfall model" of problem solving captures the essence of this linear process.

Roberts notes that simple problems enjoy a consensus on problem definition and solution. For instance, a machine breaks down on the factory floor. Through a

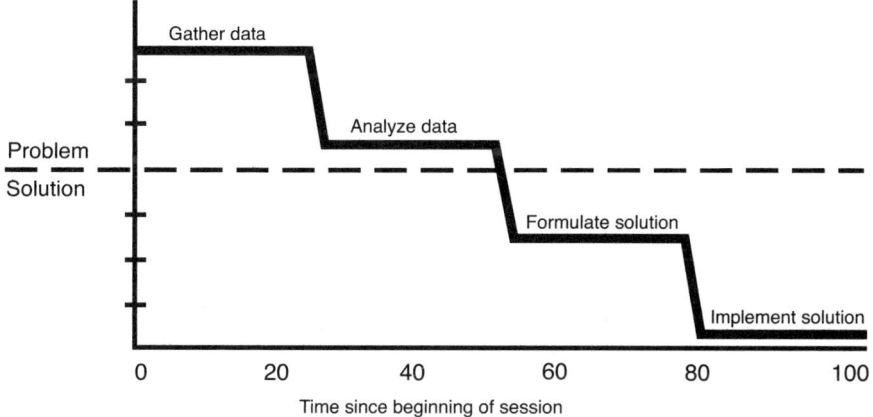

discovery and evaluation process, employees identify the problem, estimate repair cost, and provide a timeline to bring the machine back online. Along the way, employees might consider whether to airfreight the needed part or use a lower cost alternative. In relatively short order, employees gather facts by identifying the problem, analyzing the data, formulating a solution, and then implementing it.

Over 75 percent of all problems an individual or an organization encounters are simple problems. Unfortunately, simple problems can become complex if they aren't solved correctly the first time.

Consequently, most problem-solving seminars incorporate and follow a variation of this straightforward program. It's simple to teach. It's easy to grasp, implement, and quantify. And it can be optimized over time.

Complex Problems

When you introduce conflict into the problem-solving process, a second problem type commonly emerges, called a "Complex Problem." Roberts defines a complex problem as one where consensus exists on what the problem is, but there is disagreement on how to solve the problem. For instance, a company has determined that it will close a production facility, yet has decided to continue selling the product line. Stakeholders contemplate the optimum short- and long-term solutions. Should production capacity be moved to another plant? If yes, which one? Should production be outsourced to an independent vendor? Should production be moved overseas to take advantage of lower labor and production costs?

Although agreement on the problem exists, unresolved issues regarding the best solution persist. In essence, the conflict between various points of view makes the process more complex. This often leads to what is commonly referred to as "Analysis Paralysis." While a simple problem has a clearly identified solution, a complex problem will likely have multiple solutions, each proposal embraced by its respective stakeholders. Finding a solution is rarely the problem. Finding a solution that can be embraced by various stakeholders is the challenge.

Wicked Problems

Rittel and Webber identified a third problem type, which they refer to as "Wicked Problems." They realized that a unique group of problems existed outside the defined parameters of simple and complex problems. Wicked problems are special:

- There is often broad disagreement over what the problem actually is. Without an authoritative problem or statement, no definitive solution is possible.

- Since you lack definitions for both the problem and the solution, you won't know when the problem has been solved. In some instances, the problem is solved when resources are depleted, shareholders lose interest, or some other resource is exhausted, not when a perfect solution emerges.

- The problem possesses numerous implications that affect individuals in different ways. The optimum solution is less important than achieving buy-in from the community it affects.

- Solutions to wicked problems tend not to be right or wrong, but rather, better or worse. The challenge is that the evaluation process is highly subjective and the stakeholders bring their own perspective to the table.

What kind of problems might be considered wicked problems? Here are a few examples:

- You're planning a new light rail corridor. But where should it be located? What effect will the decision have on the various homeowners and communities? What effect may they have on the decision? What geological constraints and challenges exist with the various alternatives? How will each option affect the cost of the project? Which option will best serve the needs of the city in the short term and over the next 25 years or more? What unintended consequences could potentially emerge out of the various options being considered?

- Should military forces be deployed to protect a nation experiencing genocide or access to supplies of a natural resource like oil? How will the decision affect relations with adjoining countries? What will the effect be on the country itself? What unintended consequences could emerge from each potential solution? What effect would an invasion have on the political stability of the nation and the region?

As these examples illustrate, wicked problems tend to be challenging, abrasive, and highly contentious. Solutions exist, but they are potentially divisive. And a linear problem-solving approach simply doesn't seem to work in these non-linear problems. When a wicked problem exists, there tends to be winners, losers, and compromisers.

Silent Problems

Silent Problem n. A problem that is being avoided, neglected, or going unnoticed. **n.** A problem that is intentionally being silenced.

I propose a fourth problem type: the silent problem. A silent problem is one that exists, yet it lurks about unheard, often unnoticed. These problems aren't immediately obvious and may possess few visible symptoms, and at times, one can't even see them coming. At other times, these problems may be blaringly visible to those the problem affects, yet totally invisible to those who have an indirect relationship with it. Depending on where one stands, silent problems can be silent or noisy, invisible or visible.

> DEPENDING ON WHERE ONE STANDS, SILENT PROBLEMS
>
> CAN BE SILENT OR NOISY, INVISIBLE OR VISIBLE.

For leaders, a silent problem tends to be the most feared and dreaded problem of all. They're difficult to identify. At times they're chronic. From time to time, they can be malicious. And most challenging of all, leaders generally find them quite challenging to correct. For these reasons, silent problems are more likely to jeopardize an organization's future than a simple, complex, or wicked problem.

In general terms, there are three types of silent problems:

1. **Transparent Silent Problem:** In any organization there are silent problems that are easily corrected once they've been identified. For instance, I'll never forget a meeting I had with the president of a high-technology company. For months, the company had experienced numerous quality problems in its production department. In the early stages, the problem was blamed on the number of new employees on the production line. However, the problem escalated when a major client conducted an internal audit of the company and its manufacturing practices. The report card was not acceptable, so the president immediately jumped into the fray to resolve the issues. One morning, he set aside time to meet with the production team. He asked a simple question, "When a customer complaint comes to this department, what do you do with it?" The production manager looked somewhat sheepish when he responded, "We really don't know what to do with them, so we just throw them away." At this point, I can only imagine that my client saw himself in the third frame of a Dilbert cartoon with the caption, "I should have known better than to provide a wastebasket." The good news, however, is that it was easy to fix. Transparent silent problems can be identified using tools like key performance indicators (KPIs), internal audits, financial reviews, and other diagnostic instruments. Once identified, these problems can be solved using the linear process described earlier.

2. **Semi-Transparent Silent Problems**: Sometimes problems exist, but they don't look, feel, or act as if they're problems. Organizations have simply adapted and conformed to the problem over time, so the problem becomes engrained in the social environment, culture, and processes and procedures to the point where it may no longer be viewed as a problem. At other times, problems grow silent because the problem was perceived to be too complex or wicked to solve, or the resources to solve it were inadequate. Here, problems simply shrivel up on the vine, and over time are forgotten or placed on the backburner. Lastly, some semi-transparent silent problems have initiatives underway to solve them. However, due to their complexity, the problem resists change and the programs prove ineffective. In each of these instances, these silent problems might be perceived as a nuisance or possibly an irritant, but not necessarily a problem. Rather than solving it, the organization just works around it.

3. **Icebox Silent Problem**: Mankind has an inherent desire to control its destiny, even to the point of self-annihilation at times. One way is to manage problems that could be damaging or incriminating. This is accomplished by using a multitude of tactics. For instance, "a sacred cow" is a problem that commonly grows silent over time simply because it is regarded

as untouchable. Anyone who has challenged a sacred cow quickly realizes it's a win-lose proposition. Another type is commonly connected to whistleblower lawsuits and illegal activity. Through manipulation, intimidation, or a lack of transparency, the problem is placed in hush mode. Anyone who challenges that directive might be dishonored and even threatened with their life. These problems aren't being resolved. They're simply being micromanaged inside an icebox where anyone threatening to leak them are frozen out.

What is most intriguing about silent problems is they really aren't all that silent. They're only silent because they've been placed on a leash or have been placed in the freezer. Regardless of their current status, silent problems continue to live, breathe, and consume resources, and have an effect on the world around us in profound ways. And that is what makes them truly dangerous and, potentially, opportunistic!

CHAPTER

THREE

The Challenge of Silent Problems

*Companies can get into dire straits when they
ignore early signals of problems like those at
Fannie Mae and Freddie Mac.*

Robert Mittelstaedt

Problems are a core facet of human existence. Problems exist in all socio-economic strata. They know no geological or geographical boundaries. They exist in every country, every society, every community, and every household. More importantly, problems are a lens into our very being, our capacity to think, and our ability to navigate inside and outside the walls we refer to as life. To most, problems present a challenge to be solved. If we're poor at solving problems, we may not receive the promotions and recognition we deserve for years of hard work. We may not be asked to sit on an important committee, even though we would be a valuable asset.

At the other end is the fact that problems can be undisciplined. At times, they're ambiguous or sometimes deceptive. Some can be solved with the blink of an eye, while others take days, weeks, and even years to solve, and many still go unsolved. Many have significant financial consequences; others have no financial effect. Some can be solved rationally, while others become emotionally charged. Some problems are solved in advance; others not until they're created. Some take highly organized teams to solve, but others require nothing more than reading a policy manual. At times, a person who might be adept at solving a thorny problem might be totally inept at solving a routine problem. And too often, an excellent problem solver in the business arena might feel totally inept at solving problems with family, friends, and community.

Yet despite this, problems are our greatest opportunity and hope for a better world. For without problems, mankind would not find the need nor desire to invent. Our lives would be markedly different, and possibly less meaningful. Problems are at the center of our universe. And problems exist in part to be solved.

> PROBLEMS ARE OUR GREATEST OPPORTUNITY AND HOPE
>
> FOR A BETTER WORLD.

Today, many organizations use a variety of tools to detect problems early because they realize that the quicker problems can be solved, the less likely they will be to suffer harm. However, even when tools such as 360 degree assessments, key performance indicators (KPIs), and monthly financials are employed, some problems are overlooked or avoided.

When it comes to problems, outcomes are somewhat predictable:

- Simple problems tend to get solved.

- Complex problems get resolved—at least over time.

- Wicked problems are managed and at times get solved.

- Silent problems are generally neglected, at least up to the point where they begin to inflict great pain.

Why do silent problems tend to go unsolved? Because if you place silent problems under the micro-scope, you'll notice some dangerous characteristics. Silent problems often

- are undisciplined, unruly, disobedient, disruptive, and resistant to change

- contain their own set of rules, regulations, and norms

- are highly unpredictable and can be difficult to identify, quantify, and define

- contain elements of ego, bullying, tradition, and cultural norms

- are, at times, highly personal and potentially incriminating

- grow in size, morph in scope, and become virulent over time.

In addition to this list, another challenge exists. Up until now, there hasn't been a solid framework or process to expose and ultimately solve silent problems. That's why silent problems create such special challenges for leaders, challenges they may not totally understand, much less feel equipped to tackle on their own. And in this void, leaders are inclined to fight, flight, or freeze. What should we do?

Business consultant and author Pat Murray proclaims.

You stand for what you tolerate.
Define your intolerables.

Silent problems absolutely define what you tolerate. Baseball coach Yogi Bera once said, "When you come to a fork in the road, take it." A silent problem is the fork in the road. One can say, "I already have enough problems in front of me so I'm going to let my silent problems remain silent. If there are consequences from this decision, so be it. I'll deal with them." Or, one could say, "I have silent problems lurking inside my organization and I'm committed to identifying and solving them."

If you chose option one, I encourage you to simply close this book and pass it on to a colleague or friend. Maybe they'll find it useful. If you chose the second option, read on. I'll show you how to dislodge a silent problem and make it act like a real problem, one you can see and solve.

CHAPTER

FOUR

In Search of Silent Problems

The range of what we think and do is limited by what we fail to notice. And because we fail to notice that we fail to notice, there is little we can do to change until we notice that how failing to notice shapes our thoughts and deeds.

R. D. Laing

In the 1993 movie *Groundhog Day*, Bill Murray stars as Phil Connors, a TV weatherman from Pittsburgh. Connors is sent to Punxsutawney, Pennsylvania, to cover the local event known as Groundhog Day. Unexpectedly, Connors is trapped by a snowstorm, which he erroneously forecast would miss the region, and is forced to spend the night in town. When he awakes in his room the next morning, he realizes it is the morning of the day before—all over again. Everything that happened to him the previous day—the man trying to start a conversation, an old high school acquaintance who recognized him on the street, the ritual of Groundhog Day—all happens again. Day after day, Phil Connors is in a time-loop, unable to escape.

Eventually, Phil Connors' dilemma forces him to try something different. So he tries to get things right, using his knowledge of how the day will unfold to help people. For instance, he knows from previous days that a child will fall out of a tree at a certain time, and, therefore, is there to catch the child. He is granted the privilege to "get it right" by doing "the right thing."

While second chances are noteworthy and make for interesting movie plots, we rarely get second chances. You must get it right the first time. It's essential that you're able to

- provide leadership that is clear and concise

- align the team and organization for success

- earn the trust of employees, customers, creditors, and shareholders

- make good decisions under a variety of circumstances.

These are demanding requirements, even under normal circumstances. When a silent problem emerges, your challenge is heightened, the situation becomes more difficult to navigate, and your opportunity for success is diminished.

Leaders must, therefore, identify silent problems in their organizations early and act on them swiftly because the longer the problems are allowed to exist, the more entrenched they become and the more difficult they are to dislodge and solve. Time is of the essence.

> FORTUNATELY, SILENT PROBLEMS TEND NOT TO BE ALL THAT SILENT. THEY SEND OUT SIGNALS THAT SOMETHING IS WRONG.

But where do you begin the search for problems that are supposedly silent?

Fortunately, silent problems tend not to be all that silent. They send out signals that something is wrong. But unlike Phil Connors, you won't get hit repeatedly over the head. Instead, you need to be in a watchful state of awareness. With this state of mind, you will inquire, challenge, and question the status quo. But more importantly, you'll look at your world differently, enabling you to look around the corner with a fresh set of eyes.

When I went in search of silent problems, two broad themes emerged. The first theme relates to symptoms. When specific symptoms exist, there's a strong possibility that a silent problem exists. This is your first warning sign that something might be wrong, and it's time to look deeper. These yellow flag symptoms include the following:

1. When the risk of making a decision for employees inside the organization is considered to be

greater than the benefit of making one. *Symptom*: Slow and indecisive decision making.

2. When there is a willingness to embrace complexity, while simultaneously sacrificing transparency. *Symptom*: The business becomes too convoluted and complex to understand. Nothing makes sense anymore.

3. When people are prone to conforming and adapting to questionable situations too easily. *Symptom*: Everyone acts as if they're ants: busy, busy, busy. Yet nothing seems to change and few breakthroughs are achieved.

4. When information that should be readily available is difficult to access, appears incomplete, or doesn't make sense. *Symptom*: Information is delayed or incomplete, and parts often held in secrecy.

5. When internal key performance measures consistently miss their mark without a good explanation. *Symptom*: Performance standards are significantly below or over expectations.

6. When rationalization is the customary means to explain why specific targets aren't achieved or certain decisions made. *Symptom*: You don't receive a straight answer.

7. When you have that gut feeling that something isn't quite right, yet you can't put your finger on

it. *Symptom*: Queasiness in your stomach you can't explain.

These seven symptoms provide the method from which to look at your organization on a daily basis. They become the B.S. meter through which you can monitor and assess everything. If any of these symptoms surface, your first step is to search for answers and possibly a silent problem.

The second theme I identified relates to areas where silent problems are commonly found. Upon first glance, the list doesn't appear all that distinctive, silent problems often reside in areas that leaders interface with and oversee on a regular basis. Yes, they germinate, grow, and flourish right under our noses. These areas include the following:

Compensation. In my work with organizations and their CEOs, the discussion around compensation and incentive plans is common. I've seen simple plans work and thoughtful plans implode. The evidence is clear: this area is ripe for silent problems to materialize, especially if done incorrectly. W. Edwards Deming once said, "People with sharp enough targets will probably meet them, even if they have to destroy the company to do so." Unfortunately, this is what caused the 2008 mortgage crisis.

Bob Sutton, co-author of the book *Hard Facts*, writes, "The problem with using money as a motivator is that it is very difficult to get the incentive system designed so it motivates the right kind of behavior and discourages the wrong kind. You could argue that the problem with using financial incentives is that they work too well rather than not well enough—causing people to focus their attention narrowly on a small number of things and to forget more subtle and long-term issues. This is especially true with individual incentive systems."

> UNFORTUNATELY, TOO OFTEN THE BEHAVIOR YOU DESIRE
> DELIVERS AN OUTCOME YOU WEREN'T EXPECTING AND
> DIDN'T WANT.

Compensation and incentive plans are implemented to enhance business performance. The desired endpoint for every compensation and incentive plan is to drive certain types of behavior. Unfortunately, too often the behavior you desire delivers an outcome you weren't expecting and didn't want. Many of these undesirable outcomes may be of the silent variety.

Communication. Leaders realize they must lead by example, communicating a consistent message through their behavior, their actions, and their decisions. The cost of being a weak communicator for a leader or organization is immense. For instance, consider these effects of poor communications: increased workplace stress, increased turnover, high absenteeism, low morale, low productivity, increased mental health costs, and increased medical costs. When all of these potential costs are added, the effect is staggering. In today's environment, the desire to become a more effective communicator should be the goal of every person, team, department, and organization. Yet when one considers the workplace, it's apparent that ineffective communication and information overload is increasing. Despite great promise, new technologies have not lowered the bar to effective communication, but rather, they have raised it considerably.

Communication is a major source of silent problems. Here are some communication warning flags:

- inconsistent messages

- poor listening skills

- too much information is available

- communication barriers such as language exist

- communication is anxious due to strained relationships

- communication commonly contains half-truths and lies.

It's no surprise that a lack of effective communication is at the heart of many silent problems. And as we've added new communication channels, such as instant messaging, into the mix, the divide grows.

Another component of the communication challenge must not be overlooked: the role of rumors in an organization. In the absence of credible information, rumors will be generated in an attempt to make sense of it all. On the surface, rumors are undesirable, but when searching for silent problems, rumors are a channel you can leverage. Oftentimes, rumors will lead you directly to the problem and the source.

The communication challenge is summed up in the 1977 song, "The Things We Do for Love" by the group 10 CC.

Communication is the problem to the answer.

People. Leaders know their most important asset is their people! Leaders understand that "Job #1" is to lead, inspire, guide, motivate, and encourage their employees to reach new heights of achievement and success. But people are also a key reason why problems become silent or are avoided in the first place. The reasons for silence can range from deceit, to fear of speaking up.

More often than not, if a problem employee exists, that individual will affect the organization on numerous fronts. Bob Sutton explores this theme in his book, *The No Asshole Rule*. Sutton lists "The Dirty Dozen Common Everyday Actions That A**holes Use":

1. Personal insults

2. Invading one's personal territory

3. Uninvited personal contact

4. Threats and intimidation, both verbal and non-verbal

5. Sarcastic jokes and teasing used as insult delivery systems

6. Withering email flames

7. Status slaps intended to humiliate their victims

8. Public shaming or status degradation rituals

9. Rude interruptions

10. Two-faced attacks

11. Dirty looks

12. Treating people as if they are invisible.

An individual or group with toxic traits can diminish productivity, increase employee turnover, weaken communication, and increase workplace stress. Unfortunately, dealing with these issues can be challenging, so you may be tempted to avoid them, especially if these individuals have traits that are highly desirable.

> YOU'RE OFTEN CAUGHT IN A MENTAL TUG OF WAR DECIDING BETWEEN, "THIS IS WHAT I LIKE VS. THIS IS WHAT I DISLIKE ABOUT THIS PERSON."

For instance, a productive and driven salesperson is a valued asset in most organizations. But, what happens when that same individual demeans other salespeople and is in constant conflict with other departments? Do you take action and move the person out or allow the problem to fester? You're often caught in a mental tug of war deciding between, "This is what I like vs. this is what I dislike about this person." While the lines may be distinct, they're rarely conclusive. The "what I like" side of the equation frequently wins out, which means you compromise on numerous other fronts. This, in essence, becomes a problem that is visible, yet is being avoided. While you may hope that given enough time and coaching, the problem will go away, it rarely does. Leadership author Lee Thayer puts this decision-making quandary into perspective:

People will rarely trade a problem they can't stand, with a solution they can't live with.

Systems. Organizations are governed by a series of processes and procedures, rules and regulations. Processes and procedures are created from inside the organization and define how an organization does its work. Rules and regulations generally come from outside the organization. These guidelines define how the organization is to do their work and meant to prevent problems from occurring in the first place. Unfortunately, the perfect system doesn't exist.

Poor systems can be associated with everything from departmental silos to poor customer service to high employee turnover. They tend to be complex, and making sense of them can, at times, be daunting. And when a problem is present, the system generally focuses on buying time. Excuses are made regarding why it can't change or how difficult it is to change. These excuses may be true, but they should also become the warning sign that something isn't quite right. A few areas to look at include the following:

- Are there conflicts between individuals, departments, and the leadership team?

- Are denial and other defensive routines present?

- Does the organization focus on linear thinking instead of systems thinking?

- Is information used as a playing piece rather than a problem-solving tool?

- Are rigid routines and habits present?

The secret to identifying a silent problem is subtle. When things don't appear quite right, you must observe the system and challenge the status quo. And when something surfaces, don't be afraid. Instead, embrace it. Only then, can you deal with the problems and implement real change.

> THE SECRET TO IDENTIFYING A SILENT PROBLEM IS SUBTLE. WHEN THINGS DON'T APPEAR QUITE RIGHT, YOU MUST OBSERVE THE SYSTEM AND CHALLENGE THE STATUS QUO.

ISMS. In every organization, groups with specific attributes can be identified. Quite often, they have cultural underpinnings that interface with the organization. I think of these as isms, which refers to situations where momentous divides can occur. These include

- race

- gender

- generation (age group)

- sex

- class (economic)

- religion and politics.

Although process and procedures may clearly define what is acceptable and expected in these areas, this is no reason to be confident that this is how the system works. This is an area where organizations feel and are vulnerable. Allowing isms to survive and thrive should not be tolerated. However, rooting out an ism that is entrenched in an organization can be challenging. Deal with them carefully and with authority.

Summary

Our belief system regulates how we view the world and interface with it. It is and should be in a constant state of flux, simply because this place we call Earth is becoming so small and interconnected. Not surprisingly, our beliefs also regulate how we view our organizations and play an important role in determining what is really important.

One of the best defenses against silent problems is creating a culture willing to challenge the status quo and surrounding ourselves with individuals who think differently than we do. These individuals may be internal to the organization, or external. Both sources can provide a critical look; listen to them.

And, the sage old words, "If it's too good to be true, it usually is," still resonates.

FIVE

The Science behind a CAP Initiative

I've always thought that problem solving is highly overrated and that problem creation is far more interesting.

Chuck Close

As I identified in Chapter 1, the first step in most problem-solving scenarios is to identify the problem. Silent problems are no different. Without a problem, there is nothing to pursue, nothing to investigate, nothing to solve. Fortunately, silent problems tend not to be all that silent if you simply start looking for them. The first step is to identify the problem. This sounds simple, although at times it can be difficult. The challenge relates to the potential of confusing symptoms of a problem and the real problem.

Symptoms and problems are rarely identical to each other. Symptoms resemble problems at the observable level, while problems commonly reside at the hidden level. Too often, we get caught up in the emotional hyperbole of what looks like the problem when, in essence, it's only the symptom. Unless the real problem can be identified, the chance of going down the wrong path to solve a symptom is a significant risk. Separate the symptoms from the problem.

> SYMPTOMS AND PROBLEMS ARE RARELY IDENTICAL TO EACH OTHER. SYMPTOMS RESEMBLE PROBLEMS AT THE OBSERVABLE LEVEL, WHILE PROBLEMS COMMONLY RESIDE AT THE HIDDEN LEVEL.

The second challenge is the problem must be visible and perceived as worth solving. In effect, problems must have a presence. And this tends to be a point where individuals get tripped up. If an individual or a group focuses energy on solving problems that others don't believe exist, the likelihood that it will be solved is miniscule. However a problem that has presence is received in a different light. In effect, a visible problem has a storyline and a positioning statement about a potential future state.

How does one direct attention to a silent problem? The answer is quite simple, you have to awaken it. Yes, at times the best way to solve a problem is to **Create-A-Problem**, also known as a CAP initiative.

CAP initiative n. A process for solving a silent problem.

You might be saying to yourself, "This makes absolutely no sense at all." After all, an individual's perceived value to an organization is as a problem solver—not as a problem creator. In fact, individuals who create problems are generally typecast as troublemakers. If this is true, then creating a CAP initiative might appear counterpro-

> A VISIBLE PROBLEM HAS A STORYLINE AND
>
> A POSITIONING STATEMENT ABOUT A
>
> POTENTIAL FUTURE STATE.

ductive and potentially a career-damaging move.

If you came to this conclusion, you're absolutely right. Individuals are rewarded and promoted for being problem solvers. It's visible. It's honored. It's rewarded. The difference being, when problems go silent, they become invisible. And if it's perceived that no problem exists, there is nothing to solve. Consequently, a problem solver's first goal must be to make the invisible visible. And the simplest and most effective means to achieve problem visibility is to treat the existing problem as if it were a new problem. Giving the problem a fresh perspective, a renewed emphasis and an innovative position—in essence, a CAP initiative.

There are several important differences between a traditional problem-solving sequence and that of a CAP initiative (Table 5.1). In a traditional problem-solving scenario, the dialogue and progression surrounding the problem is an open-book process. In essence, individuals who need to be in the know are kept abreast of the problem and the progress toward solving it. This open-book policy is present from the moment a problem is identified to the point a solution is in place. In a CAP initiative, silence is an integral part of the process. For instance, from the moment a problem is identified to the minute the solution is presented, the CAP initiative is in a silent lock-down mode. Only a select few are involved in the identification and formulation stages of the CAP initiative. The initiative becomes open when the CAP solution is presented, which is late in the process. This changes the dynamics of the problem, and how it's received, perceived, and solved.

Table 5.1

Traditional Problem Solving	CAP Initiative Problem Solving
Identify Problem (Open)	Identify Problem (Silent)
Gather Data (Open)	Formulate Solution (Silent)
Analyze Data (Open)	Present CAP Solution (Open)
Formulate Solution (Open)	Gather Feedback (Open)
Implement Solution (Open)	Pursue, Refine, and Implement Solution (Open)

Here's an example of how a CAP initiative works. In the 1990s, Continental Airlines was struggling and its customer-service ratings were amongst the lowest in the industry. Gordon Bethune and Greg Brenneman were brought in as CEO and president to fix the ailing airline. Prior to their arrival, the bankers and lawyers were running the company by the book. If an employee provided a benefit for a customer that was considered unacceptable, it was documented and a rule documenting what the proper action should have been was created. Over the years, the rules were accumulated into a book that grew nine inches thick and was known as the *Thou Shalt Not* book. There were so many rules that no one could possibly know them all, so employees played it safe by doing nothing at all. Customer service quickly evolved into a theory, not a practice, and customers were left to fend for themselves. Although almost everyone inside Continental knew the book was a problem, the problem was generally silent. It was easier to accept it, than fight it.

Under normal circumstances, corporate manuals take years to create using a process of refinement and updating, which makes it easy to add to and difficult to delete from. However, this story is different. Bethune and Brenneman quickly identified the problem. Now they had to do something BIG, something memorable. They sent out a notice to the employees at headquarters with instructions to meet in the parking lot at a specified time. When the employees arrived, a surprise awaited them. There, in the middle of the parking lot was a fifty-five-gallon drum. As employees watched, Bethune and Brenneman tossed the *Thou Shalt Not* book into the fifty-five-gallon drum and poured gasoline over it. And with the simple strike of a match, the book went up in flames. Hundreds of employees stood in awe, realizing from that moment forward their jobs were going to change.

Bethune and Brenneman then anchored their point when they said, "Continental Airlines is your company to make great. Go do it—Now!"

For some, the book was likely a kindred friend, since it really simplified their job. After all, a do-nothing position was easy to embrace. For others, the burning created an opportunity to do what was right for the customer and the company. With that simple yet profound act, management's bold statement made the invisible visible. First, it demonstrated that the new management team understood the silent problem and they were ready to tackle it head on. Second, it recognized that management had helped create the problem by constructing too many rules and regulations and they were ready to help solve it. Third, the new management team was granting permission to its employees to act in the best interest of Continental Airlines. And fourth, it made the new vision, soon to be announced, visible and memorable. Customer-service ratings improved immediately.

The incredible results Continental Airlines achieved are a testament to how important it is to make the invisible visible. The employees were likely saying, "Wow, these guys get it. They actually understand what goes on inside our organization." When this occurs, the trust quotient escalates immediately, which in turn can be leveraged toward bigger and better initiatives.

A CAP initiative is a tool developed specifically to tackle and solve silent problems. Its purpose is twofold. The first is to make the problem visible to the intended audience. The second is to have the intended audience take action to solve the problem. This is achieved using a non-traditional method. Normally, one would raise his or her hand and say, "We have a problem over here and I think we need to talk about it." At this point, people can simply disregard the cry for help, stating it's not worth their time or effort, or they can debate the problem, whether or not it truly exists or if it's really important. A CAP initiative creates a sense of urgency around the problem by pushing forth a solution, which completely bypasses the problem-identification stage.

It's been my experience that

> *People identify with problems, but they become attached to solutions.*

When you present a solution, individuals are compelled to interact with it either in a positive, negative, or unsettled manner. For instance, when Bethune and Brenneman burned the *Thou Shalt Not* book, there was no ambiguity about how they felt about the book. However, individual employee reaction could vary depending on how they felt it affected them personally. The solution (destroying the book) then became the point of reference rather than the problem. This reoriented the problem and how individuals interfaced with it.

Once you launch a CAP initiative, you've immediately placed the problem in the spotlight for others to see. And what do they see? If you're successful, they see a simple problem—one challenging enough to get their interest, yet not too challenging to scare them off. And that's why positioning a silent problem in simple terms can be a critical step in creating a CAP initiative. For instance, the Continental Airlines story from the inside probably looked quite complex. After all, a nine-inch book of rules and regulations took years to develop, and with that comes complexity. And complexity can lead directly to analysis paralysis. Simplicity promotes forward progress. And what makes the Continental Airlines story so profound is its simplicity.

A second factor is critically important. People, in general like to help solve problems, and I call these individuals problem responders. Problem responders are individuals like you and me. They come from all walks of life, and they want to make a difference. They don't necessarily need to be in a lead role. In fact, most of the time, they simply want to participate and play the role of a supporter. If you create a CAP initiative, individuals will likely join in to solve the problem. Problem responders become excited about a problem if

- it aligns with their personal values

- they believe in the cause and its leader(s)

- they believe the solution is achievable.

For instance, natural disasters like forest fires, tornadoes, and earthquakes affect millions of individuals and thousands of communities around the world each year. And amazingly, when the victims of these disasters ask for help, people step forward in droves. Some provide money, while others provide labor, shelter, or tools. For their hard work, they receive immense personal satisfaction and maybe a free sandwich. They simply want to help. They are disaster responders.

> PROBLEM RESPONDERS ARE INDIVIDUALS LIKE YOU AND
> ME. THEY COME FROM ALL WALKS OF LIFE, AND THEY
> WANT TO MAKE A DIFFERENCE.

Problem responders are similar, and often the same individuals. They simply want to help. They want to be part of a cause they can support and endorse. They look to these challenges as opportunities to improve the status quo. They look at problems from a social context, which enables them to become an integral part of the community and the brand. And they often become viral agents for the cause. Problem responders are the army for change and hope, especially when it comes to tackling problems once they've been awakened.

A CAP initiative identifies a silent problem and awakens it. It becomes a brand and a catalyst for change. It engages problem responders to find and implement a solution. And it positions the problem around a cause that others can embrace. Yes, silent problems could be your organization's greatest opportunity.

II

How CAP
Initiatives Work

SIX

The Zones

I see better now as a blind man than as a sighted man.
I discovered we don't see with our eyes. We only see
when we are willing to look at the truth about us, life
and other people. You don't need eyes to see that.

from the movie *At First Sight*

Silent problems don't respond to general problem-solving protocol. In fact, at times applying typical problem-solving tools to silent problems can make matters worse. What's needed is fresh thinking, along with new and innovative problem-solving techniques. Consider Alfred Nobel and his discovery of dynamite. Nobel was introduced to nitroglycerine at a young age, and at the time, nitroglycerine was considered to be too dangerous to be of any practical use since it was extremely sensitive to shock and difficult to predict under what conditions it might explode. In one of Nobel's many breakthroughs,

he discovered a way to absorb nitroglycerine onto kiesel-
guhr (a diatomaceous earth that Nobel initially found in
the German moorlands). This breakthrough enabled him
to form a paste, which was easy to knead and shape, creating dynamite. This new form was more stable and could
be transported and subjected to jolts without exploding.

But this created yet another problem. Now that
dynamite was stable, how to ignite it and thereby achieve
ignition? This forced Nobel to invent yet another product, which he called a blasting cap. A blasting cap simply
creates a small explosion that triggers a larger explosion
in the dynamite itself.

Interestingly, silent problems can be every bit as
unpredictable as that of nitroglycerine back in the 1850s.
But what would happen if we took a page out of Alfred
Nobel's playbook? What would happen if one could
transform a silent problem so it looked like and behaved
like a real problem? And what would happen if one could
construct a blasting cap to ignite the problem, leading
to a new and innovative solution? Would this create the
breakthrough discovery we seek?

I applied fresh thinking to silent problems and discovered the CAP initiative process. It was every bit as
profound and innovative as Nobel's blasting cap. It's simple. It's impact, profound.

Peter Senge, founder of the Center for Organizational Learning at MIT's Sloan School of Business and
author of *The Fifth Discipline,* begins to connect the dots to
why a CAP initiative works under such varied and challenging conditions. Senge writes:

In creating, we seek to make what we truly care about exist.

When we create a CAP initiative, we proclaim what we truly care about—and work hard to make it exist— the blasting cap, so to speak. We achieve this by either putting forward a solution or by creating a situation that exposes and highlights the problem. This runs counter to an individual's instinct. We're programmed to believe that our first action is to identify the problem, which is to profess, "I believe we have a problem and here it is.... What do you think?" When you use this tactic on a silent problem, the likely outcome will be disagreement, confrontation, or avoidance, thereby delaying action by doing nothing, creating a committee, or putting forth misleading information. However, when you present a solution, the problem is likely to garner attention, which is the first step in solving a silent problem. If you are successful, the problem will come to life. And along the way, the problem will be infused with structure, so it behaves more predictably, more like that of a regular problem.

Once you launch a CAP initiative, a second element begins to take form, the problem identification aspect of the equation. Senge also writes:

In problem solving, we seek to make something we do not like go away.

Since the CAP initiative presents a solution, it forces the target audience to respond. You must be tuned in to this activity because it provides the first glimpse into how recipients perceive the situation and the problem itself. Do they agree or disagree? Do they take a position of action or avoidance? Do they honor the situation or attempt to minimize it? How they act and react is critically important in understanding the silent problem and whom it's important to. With this insight, you can decide the next step, which can be placed into one of three distinct zones:

- **Aligned Zone.** The Aligned Zone is the end game; the point where the CAP initiator and the CAP recipient agree on both the framework of the problem and the solution. In essence, it's the green light to pursue the solution as defined by the CAP initiative. Although reaching this point is the desired outcome for every CAP initiative, achieving it directly out of the blocks is infrequent. However, as we learned in the Continental Airlines *Thou Shall Not* story, it can happen.

- **BOILS Zone.** This stands for **B**artering **O**ver **I**deas, **L**ogic, and **S**olutions. As the acronym implies, in this zone people generate and find solutions. Under most scenarios, the CAP recipient will admit that a problem exists, yet might disagree with all, or part of the solution. This is not a defeat, but rather a victory, since the silent problem is now visible. And once the problem is visible, the initiator and recipient of the CAP initiative work toward a solution that can be mutually agreed upon and deployed.

- **Contentious Zone.** At times, the target audience of a CAP initiative not only disagrees with the solution/situation, but also advocates that a problem doesn't even exist. When the recipient enters the Contentious Zone, the potential for a prolonged battle increases significantly. You might decide the risks are too high and it just isn't worth the fight. Or your passion to pursue the problem will kick in, and you'll discover you can move mountains. However, it may take time.

Regardless of which option the targeted CAP recipients pursue, they expose their position, providing the first glimpse into how they perceive the situation and, in turn, how one needs to move forward. If they're in the Aligned Zone, it's full steam ahead. If the CAP recipients fall into the BOILS Zone, progress is likely, however, they'll need to do some degree of bartering along the way, and an altered solution is probable. And if they're in the Contentious Zone, they're likely to fight you every step of the way, hoping to keep the problem silent.

Whatever zone the CAP recipients falls into, their problem-solving juices will kick in. Remember, any action is a step toward making the problem become visible and, ultimately, finding a solution. And once you know how the targeted audience responds, the anatomy of your silent problem is defined.

> THE CAP INITIATIVE RESETS THE SILENT PROBLEM, RESETS THE QUESTIONS, AND BEGINS TO RESET THE BEHAVIORS AND ACTIONS OF THE PARTICIPANTS.

The CAP initiative resets the silent problem, resets the questions, and begins to reset the behaviors and actions of the participants. Eventually, a problem that was ambiguous and formless becomes tangible. And what was previously invisible to most becomes visible to everyone.

The best way to understand the CAP initiative process and how to use it in your organization is through examples. The next five chapters present vivid examples of how to identify and resolve silent problems in your organization.

From the Bottom Up
Silent Problem Type—Semi-Transparent

ALIGNED ZONE

Given the right circumstances, from no more than dreams, determination and the liberty to try, people consistently do extraordinary things.

Dee Hock, *Birth of the Chaordic Age*

When we hear the words, "once upon a time," instinctively we sit up straight, for what is to come must be important. Without further instruction, everyone in the room stops what they're doing and listens intently for the story that follows.

In real life, getting attention can be a daunting task. Oftentimes, it's the difference between success and failure. For C-Level executives, getting attention is often expected and taken for granted. Employees lower in the organization, however, often find it difficult to achieve, often complicated by gender, race, and other societal divides. Take a recent corporate-wide initiative underway inside Best Buy, the multinational consumer electronics giant based in Minneapolis, Minnesota.

Brad Anderson started his career with Best Buy as a sales associate in a St. Paul store, then promoted to CEO in 2002. Shortly after his promotion to CEO, Anderson led an initiative to transition Best Buy from an excellent product delivery company to what he termed a "customer centricity" business. The goal of the new strategic direction was to serve the company's most profitable customers. Anderson and his team identified six key customer segments, one referred to as the berry customer. The berry customer possessed the distinct characteristics of having too much money, too little time, and found technology to be too complex.

Julie Gilbert was brought in to identify key strategies that fit the needs of this customer segment and turn these concepts into products. She became co-lead of Best Buy's Magnolia Home Theatre store-within-a-store concept. She shared her responsibilities equally with Dean, her male counterpart. Together, they were responsible for setting up and deploying the concept across the vast network of Best Buy stores.

This story starts the day Julie was readying to launch a new Magnolia Home Theatre store in California. A significant publicity event was planned with Brad Anderson and Chairman of the Board Dick Schultz, along with several other board members. When Julie arrived at the store the day prior to the event, Lindsey, a store employee, asked Julie for help. Lindsey had never presented to such a high-profile group before and was concerned, so she asked if Julie could help her with her presentation. Julie agreed.

They walked down to a nearby Starbucks to review her presentation. After a couple of hours, Lindsey's presentation was ready for prime time. But then the conversation turned in an unanticipated direction. Lindsey said, "Julie, you just don't get it. What you don't get is that we don't fit here. We don't fit in this company, and we don't fit in this industry." Lindsey meant that women simply didn't fit in the male-dominant technology sector, which included working for Best Buy.

Unfortunately, Julie understood those words all too well because she had lived them herself. For she, too, had become aware of the male-dominant culture inside the organization. When she visited stores, it was quickly evident that her stature at corporate was greatly diminished at the retail level. She recalls, "When I visited stores with Dean, eye contact and conversation quickly went to him, not me. I would stand next to him trying to say, 'Hey, I'm Julie, I'm right here.'" She realized she was invisible in the eyes of the male-dominant culture inside the store, despite being an equal on the organizational chart.

This wasn't easy to accept, and Julie soon discovered that these cultural underpinnings weren't unique to her. They affected every aspect of Best Buy's business, from the number of women job applicants, to the turnover percentage of women at the store level, to the input women were having on marketing and advertising campaigns. And more importantly, these issues didn't come to a screeching halt at the employee level; they traveled all the way down to the total customer experience. Basically corporate culture said, if you want to sell a really cool system, the salesperson needed to talk to the man of the household. To Julie, these were red flags.

Imagine for a minute that you were challenged with a similar scenario. What types of questions would you begin to formulate and ask? What types of information would you seek? What would you do next?

In most instances, this is where the story stops, and no happily ever after ending exists. It ends quietly, with barely a whimper. And nothing changes. The problem remains silent. However, this story is different. If there was ever an invitation to make a difference, this was it. And the next step Julie took was unorthodox. It was daring. It was risky. She was frustrated and inspired at the same time.

Julie's inspiration occurred at 2 AM, weeks after her conversation with Lindsey. She was thinking about her meeting with Lindsey and its various implications. Eventually, her thoughts turned to her growing up on a farm in rural South Dakota. This is where she learned to respect and admire every aspect of the wolf ecosystem. It was then that a bolt of lightening struck, when she asked herself, "If not me, who is going to do this?"

Shortly thereafter, she started her journey by contacting several women she knew inside Best Buy on the West Coast. She asked each to meet her at the Fairmont in Santa Clara on Friday morning.

When Friday came, Julie laid out the problem, the opportunity, and the vision. Were they willing to commit? If yes, Julie was willing to head up the initiative and figure out how to finance it with her personal budget. Everyone was on board and agreed that the ball must move forward. The initiative would be called WOLF (Women's Leadership Forum). They'd form independent "wolf packs" consisting of twenty-five women and two men, and they'd mirror the structure found in the wild, where each pack would be a family unit, loyal to each other with its own leadership structure. The wolf-pack concept would be based on three-core pillars:

1. **Commitment**: A commitment to each other and a commitment to innovate the business.

2. **Network**: Helping each member create a network that could authentically help change the company.

3. **Give Back**: Give back to the community, which inevitably means giving hope to those one might touch every day, inside and outside of the organization.

Over the following days and weeks, WOLF took form, despite still being a secret inside Best Buy. Brad Anderson recounts the meeting when Julie informed him of WOLF and the passion she held for it. When Anderson greeted Julie, he sensed that something was wrong, saying, "I've been through these circumstances before and I knew I was going to hear some sort of an ultimatum."

After a short pause, Julie entered Anderson's office where she delivered the vision she held for WOLF and its place inside Best Buy. The idea for WOLF struck Anderson as being, "highly eccentric, very unusual and brilliant." Anderson further realized that WOLF would be "incredibly contentious, because anything that matters is."

Julie then placed her ultimatum on the table, "If you don't do it. I'm leaving."

Why the Initiative Worked

In the beginning, the vision of doing the right thing for women employees, women customers, and Best Buy was a driving force. However, as could be expected, making a sustainable difference in an organization the size of Best Buy can be a daunting task. After all, the old saying "culture kills change almost every time" holds true. In spite of the odds, the initiative broke through, and in 2003, WOLF became a fully funded initiative inside Best Buy. Over time, new wolf packs formed. New leadership opportunities presented themselves. And the once male-dominated culture changed forever.

By 2007, WOLF achieved several milestones, according the Best Buy's 2007 Corporate Responsibility Report:

- In areas with wolf packs, there had been a 5.7 percent reduction in female turnover, with the savings alone covering the costs of the WOLF program.

- The number of female general managers in U.S. stores had increased 40 percent, and the number of female sales managers by 100 percent.

- WOLF leadership has become integral in every aspect of Best Buy's business, from general marketing to store layouts and new services.

- The number of female Geek Squad employees had increased 284 percent in just three years.

Today, WOLF is integrated into every aspect of the Best Buy organization. It touches everything from hiring to retention to the total customer experience. It's having a huge bottom line effect. It, in effect, has become a competitive advantage. The culture, the turnover rate among women, and the lack of respect for women, including customers, were the symptoms of the problem. The problem was really about respecting women in the workforce and honoring the buying power of women in today's society.

WHEN ONE GOES DOWN THE PATH OF A CAP INITIATIVE, THERE TENDS TO BE AN IGNITION POINT, THE POINT WHERE THE FUMES OF DESIRE UNITE WITH THE SPARK OF DESPERATE HOPE.

When one goes down the path of a CAP initiative, there tends to be an ignition point, the point where the fumes of desire unite with the spark of desperate hope.

It's at this point where mankind can conquer massive tasks and solve some of its most challenging problems.

Julie and her co-creators of WOLF showed remarkable insight into how to create a CAP initiative. They identified a problem but sold a solution. The solution became a brand that everyone could identify with and wanted to be a part of. They created a vision that embraced the individual and supported the goals of the organization.

Today, WOLF succeeds on a passion and a vision for a new and vibrant future. It succeeds because individuals are willing to put some skin in the game. It succeeds because it captures the imaginations of the people—women and men alike.

—The Masters Forum. September 11, 2007.
Presenters: Julie Gilbert and Brad Anderson.
Title: *How to get there from here—Winning with Women—WOLF"*

EIGHT

The Head Fake
Silent Problem Type — Semi-Transparent

BOILS ZONE

The best collective decisions are the product of disagreement and contest, not consensus and compromise.

James Surowiecki, *The Wisdom of Crowds*

We can all agree that respected business leaders should be adept at solving problems, not necessarily creating them. At least that's what I thought until I met Barbara one summer day. Barbara is an entrepreneur with a knack for getting things done. Because she runs a tight ship, her company is a consistent performer on every business metric, from sales to profitability. So when Barbara told me her story, I was surprised at the process she used and the remarkable outcome.

Barbara had grown increasingly frustrated with incessant infighting amongst her senior management team, lack of cooperation, wrestling for resources, and a general lack of teamwork. The issue was becoming a silent problem that everyone was adapting to. Over several months, Barbara worked with her team searching for solutions, but they simply were unable to cross the chasm they so desperately needed to cross.

As she pondered the situation, she realized she needed 100 percent buy-in by every member of the management team and 100 percent commitment to the solution. They had to own the outcome.

As a traditional problem solver, Barbara knew how to fix the problem. She had watched and analyzed the inner workings of her team for months, and her desired solution was straightforward. However, she also knew that if she implemented her solution, there would be a backlash. Her vision to achieve 100 percent buy in and 100 percent commitment would be in jeopardy. Barbara's challenge was to create a solution they owned.

Throughout the day, Barbara pulled together her ideas and crafted an email that first stated the problem. Then she suggested a solution and set a meeting for 10:00 AM the following morning to discuss the solution. She waited until the end of the day as members of her team were leaving for home before pushing the "Send" button.

At this point, this is pretty standard stuff. However, the solution that Barbara proposed was a head fake, enticing her team to create an alternate solution, one they could support and endorse. Indeed, the solution Barbara proposed in her email would have actually made things worse. However, she was confident her team would discover the flawed proposal and create an alternative.

Barbara had launched a CAP initiative as a means to solving a problem.

When Barbara arrived at 10:00 AM the following morning, everyone was in the conference room talking among themselves. Barbara sat down at the head of the table and said, "Does anyone have any comments or suggestions regarding this plan?"

When Barbara stopped, Kelly raised her hand. "Barbara, we were wondering if you would be open to an alternative plan?"

Barbara responded, "Of course I am...."

For the next 45 minutes, the discussion was focused and right on target. Her team was prepared to "Barter Over Ideas, Logic, and Solutions." They were in the BOILS Zone. By the end of the discussion, they put in place the solution that Barbara had envisioned all along. But since she made them solve her create-a-problem challenge, they owned the solution. Within days, her team started to work as a high-performance team once again. It was seamless and almost effortless.

As Barbara told me her story, I was struck by the brilliance of her strategy and the remarkable outcome. What could have taken months to fix using a normal problem-solving process, took less than 24 hours to identify and implement. Barbara had successfully executed a CAP initiative instinctively.

CAP Initiative Overview

Composer and filmmaker Robert Fritz once wrote, "If you limit your choices only to what seems possible or reasonable, you disconnect yourself from what you truly want, and all that is left is compromise." And when it comes to problem solving, our basic instinct is to fix the problem, which quite often is only a compromise. It's that simple and that difficult. In essence:

In creating, we seek to make what we truly care about exist.

For Barbara, it would have been simple to solve the problem. She knew exactly how to fix the problem. But it was the gap between solution and implementation that concerned her most. She knew her team, and she needed a solution they could embrace and be eager to implement quickly.

However, due to the challenge and constraints of the situation, Barbara was forced to think and act differently. She had to focus on the desired outcome, what she truly wanted. For a problem solver, this is quite challenging. Therefore, from the moment she focused on dealing with the problem, she, in turn, was pushed into thinking outside the box.

> IT WAS THE GAP BETWEEN SOLUTION AND IMPLEMENTA-
> TION THAT CONCERNED HER MOST.

Barbara's solution also begs a question. Would a more traditional top-down solution approach have also worked? A standard answer would be, "It depends." Every situation is different. Every team is different. Every scenario is different. In this instance, Barbara hit a brick wall with a traditional approach and had to break down that brick wall.

When Barbara told me her story, I realized it defied the tried and true principles of every management book written. It placed the trust quotient so critical to effective leadership in jeopardy. And yes, the strategy to get her management team reenergized could have easily backfired. However, similar situations do occur, and extreme measures at times must be considered.

> EVERY ONCE IN A WHILE LET YOUR TEAM SOLVE ITS THORNIEST PROBLEMS.

The optimal solution for any given problem is dependent upon numerous internal and external factors. Factors such as culture, management style, experience, and urgency are but a few of the elements that will weigh in this equation. At the very least, one must consider how to best solve a given problem. Many leaders have succeeded by being excellent problem solvers, but sometimes being a strong problem solver can get in the way. Every once in a while let your team solve its thorniest problems. Don't overlook the philosophy, "people embrace what they help create."

CHAPTER

NINE

The Cause
Silent Problem Type—Semi-Transparent

CONTENTIOUS ZONE

Power concedes nothing without a demand. It never did, and it never will. Find out just what people will submit to, and you have found out the exact amount of injustice and wrong, which will be imposed upon them; and this will continue till they have resisted with either words or blows, or with both. The limits of tyrants are prescribed by the endurance of those who they suppress.

Frederick Douglas, abolitionist, 1849

Some stories lead us to believe in fairy tales because fairy tales, on occasion, come true. This story's roots are found in fairy tales like Cinderella, Little Red Riding Hood, and Snow White. And along the journey, individuals are elevated and, ultimately, transformed. What was once tolerated became the birthmark of intolerance. What was taken for granted became highly contentious, and in the end, the fairest of them all was chosen, and her name was Rosa Parks.

This story begins in the early 1950s when Fred Gray, during his junior year in college at Alabama State University, made a commitment to pursue a degree in law, become a lawyer, then return to his hometown of Montgomery, Alabama, and destroy everything segregated he could find. However, this would be no simple task. For instance, he was unable to pursue a law degree at the University of Alabama since it was segregated at the time. Instead, Gray enrolled at Case Western University in Cleveland, where at the age of twenty-three, he finished his schooling, passed his bar exam for the state of Ohio, and then six weeks later received his license to practice law in Alabama. Gray returned to Montgomery and set up his law practice, one of only two black attorneys in the city.

Gray was already familiar with the leaders of the civil rights movement. This included noteworthy leaders like E. D. Nixon, who was the head of the Montgomery branch of the Pullman Porters and president of the local National Association for the Advancement of Colored People (NAACP); Jo Ann Robinson, president of the Women's Political Council, the largest and most active black civic organization in Montgomery; and Clifford Durr, a white lawyer, who along with his wife, Virginia, were civil rights activists. Gray had also become a close friend of Rosa Parks, who worked as a seamstress at the Montgomery Fair department store and was also the secretary to the Montgomery branch of the NAACP and served as its youth director.

At that time, the ill treatment of blacks on Montgomery buses was a potentially explosive problem. Buses were segregated with the front ten rows permanently reserved for white passengers, while blacks were required to sit in the last ten rows. Black passengers were allowed to sit in a reserved section of seats in the middle section of the bus, but if a white passenger needed a seat, blacks were obligated to move from this section. These rules, while generally honored, were a persistent irritant amongst blacks, especially since so many blacks depended on bus transportation.

On March 2, 1955, just six months after Gray's return to Montgomery, he received a call from Claudette Colvin, a fifteen-year-old African-American student from the Booker T. Washington High School. She had boarded a city bus, sat in the middle section of the bus, and refused to give up her seat to a white man. Colvin was subsequently handcuffed, arrested, and dragged from the bus. She was charged with violating the state segregation law, disorderly conduct, and resisting arrest. At the time of the arrest, Colvin was active in the NAACP's youth council and was advised by none other than Rosa Parks. Fred Gray would represent Colvin in juvenile court in Montgomery County.

Following Colvin's arrest, Gray and several civil rights organizations met with city and bus officials, threatening to launch a bus boycott. But because Colvin was several months pregnant, Nixon and Gray decided she was an unsuitable symbol for their cause. Instead, the black community needed an upstanding candidate of unimpeachable character, one who could withstand the scrutiny of the courts and the press.

Seven months later, on October 21, 1955, eighteen-year-old Mary Louise Smith was arrested for not relinquishing her seat, again in the middle section of the bus, this time to a white woman. Black leaders considered her as a test case but declined because it was rumored that her father was an alcoholic.

December 1, 1955, was just like any other day for Gray. He went to his law firm, and then at noon he had lunch with his friend Rosa Parks. Following lunch, he traveled to an out-of-town appointment. When he returned home later that evening, he learned that Parks had been arrested for disorderly conduct on the Cleveland Avenue bus. Parks had been seated in the first row in the middle section of the bus—the non-segregated section. At the third stop in front of the Empire Theater, a white man boarded the bus and was forced to stand because the first 10 rows were already taken. The bus driver informed Parks and the other three passengers seated in that row to vacate their seats for the white passenger. Three passengers moved, but Parks remained seated. The bus driver called the police, and when they arrived they promptly arrested Parks, and took her into police custody. She was charged with "refusing to obey orders of a bus driver."

After Parks was released on bail, Fred Gray, E. D. Nixon, Clifford Durr, and his wife Virginia met Parks and her husband in their apartment. The group decided Rosa Parks would be the ideal plaintiff for a test case. She was above moral reproach, a civic and religious worker, politically savvy, and well respected in the black community, and she possessed a quiet fortitude. Despite her husband's opposition, Rosa Parks agreed to become a test case. She asked Fred Gray to be her attorney.

Later that evening, Nixon told Jo Ann Robinson what had happened earlier in the day. Robinson convened an emergency meeting of the Women's Political Council, and they decided to kick off the long-discussed boycott of city buses on their own. She spent the night mimeographing 35,000 half-page flyers to distribute at black schools and throughout black neighborhoods the following day. The notice stated, "We are, therefore, asking every Negro to stay off the buses Monday in protest of the arrest and trial. Don't ride the buses to work, to town, to school...."

Monday came and despite the threat of rain, 40,000 people stayed off the buses, with some walking up to twenty miles or more. Rosa Parks appeared in court for a thirty-minute trial and was convicted and fined. Later that afternoon, the Montgomery Improvement Association (MIA) was formed. There a relative newcomer was elected their president, Martin Luther King Jr. That evening, the MIA held a meeting at the Holt Street Baptist Church to decide the future direction of the protest and to call upon blacks to continue the boycott. They then negotiated with city and bus officials during December and January, proposing a more liberal seating arrangement, which the parent bus company was using in Mobile and other southern cities. Montgomery city and bus officials refused to accept MIA's demands.

On January 30, 1956, the MIA Executive Board decided to file a federal lawsuit to challenge the constitutionality of the city and state bus segregation statutes. On February 1, Fred Gray and Charles Langford filed the federal lawsuit on behalf of four African-American women: Aurelia S. Browder, Susie McDonald, Claudette Colvin, and Mary Louise Smith. Gray decided not to include Rosa Parks in the case to avoid the perception that they were seeking to circumnavigate her prosecution. Gray wanted only one issue for the courts to decide: the constitutionality of the laws requiring segregation on buses.

The case was tried on June 5 in the U.S. District Court for the Middle District of Alabama. The three-judge district court ruled two to one that segregation on Alabama's intrastate buses was unconstitutional. The defendants appealed directly to the U.S. Supreme Court, which on November 13 affirmed the district court's decision. On December 17, the Supreme Court rejected city and state appeals to reconsider the decision. On December 20, after 381 days, the Reverend Martin Luther King Jr. officially called off the boycott, and the following morning, Montgomery buses were integrated.

Why Rosa Parks Remained Seated

Action is eloquence.
William Shakespeare

According to the Alabama Department of Archives and History, "Parks'" arrest was set in motion following several years of planning for such an event by the local civil rights organizations and civic groups." The Women's Political Council, a civic group composed of black women professionals, had considered a boycott of the city's buses before Parks' arrest. What the Council and black leaders like E. D. Nixon needed, however, was a black passenger whose arrest would engender a citywide boycott of Montgomery's buses. Essentially, the problem was identified and a strategy in place. All they needed was their leading actor or actress to appear.

Parks became that lead actress. Her image in the black community was respected. Her knowledge of the busing situation was high. Her ability to galvanize the African-American community into a bus boycott appeared plausible. Her convictions regarding the ongoing racial injustice in Montgomery made her a person they believed they could base a protest on.

Until December 1, 1955, several opportunities had presented themselves, but none had withstood the character test. Parks had the right stuff. In addition, Parks, being an active participant in the civil rights movement and interested in a bus boycott, was well prepped and versed about what to do if by chance it were she. For instance, interviews disclose that she knew that if she ever was evicted from a bus: "don't frown, don't struggle, don't shout, and don't pay the fine."

When asked about the incident in a 1956 interview that aired on radio station KPFA, Parks said, "The time had just come when I had been pushed as far as I could stand to be pushed, I suppose. They placed me under arrest. And I wasn't afraid. I don't know why I wasn't, but I didn't feel afraid. I had decided that I would have to know once and for all what rights I had as a human being and a citizen, even in Montgomery, Alabama."

Why the CAP Initiative Was Successful

It wasn't about starting a movement. It was a matter of trying to correct a wrong that existed. And this was a part of correcting the wrong. It developed into the movement. What happened in Mrs. Parks' situation and after she was arrested was a calculated plan to organize, develop and have a bus boycott. None of us knew if it was going to work out at the time, but we were willing to make the effort.

Fred Gray Sr.

When you contemplate a CAP initiative, remember that one size does not fit all. Often, a CAP initiative is proactive, with every piece in its place, every detail considered, and every intersection on the time line plotted. At other times, the heroes remain unknown until the last second, and when they appear, they surface from out of the blue and rise instantaneously to meteoric heights.

In the instance of the Montgomery bus boycott, this was a story waiting patiently for decades to happen. It's a story of oppression, hostility, and anger. It's a story that illustrates the unreceptive character of initiatives that reside in the Contentious Zone. It's a story partially written, anxiously waiting for Prince Charming (in this case a princess) to appear. And when the princess came forth, she became a catalyst for change and unity that would be heard around the world.

The Montgomery bus boycott can attribute its success to numerous individuals and many factors. At the very least, black leaders realized the risks were high for undertaking such an event. They realized that if they were going to change the racial landscape, the black community would need to come together, becoming fully enfranchised. There was very little room for error, and the potential for the situation to grow out of control, a possibility.

The Montgomery bus boycott will be remembered as one of the most successful citizen movements in history. The most distinguishing characteristic was its non-violent nature. Today, civil rights movements surface around the globe with great regularity, many include violence and many suffer casualties. When force is employed, the side that possesses the capacity to exert the greatest force wins. CAP initiatives focus on using power, not force. And in the end, power usually wins.

> WHEN FORCE IS EMPLOYED, THE SIDE THAT POSSESSES THE CAPACITY TO EXERT THE GREATEST FORCE WINS. CAP INITIATIVES FOCUS ON USING POWER, NOT FORCE.

TEN

The Challenge
Silent Problem Type—Ice Box

BOILS ZONE

Genius can be more accurately identified by perserver-ance, courage, concentration, enormous drive, and abso-lute talent—talent alone is certainly not enough.

David R. Hawkins, M.D., Ph.D.

Today, Alfred Nobel is renowned for the establishment of his philanthropic foundation, The Nobel Prize. However, when Nobel's will was read following his death on December 10, 1896, it created nothing but havoc. Alfred Nobel had "Created a Problem" of immense proportions, the equivalent of a blasting cap setting off a stick of dynamite, both Nobel inventions. It created a shockwave across Sweden and parts of the world for these seven reasons:

1. Alfred Nobel drew up his own will, which
    was flawed and legally deficient in many areas.
    For instance, challenges relating to his legal
    residence surfaced. Nobel owned residences in
    many countries and had never established legal
    residence. For many years, he resided in France,
    although he died at his villa in Italy.

2. Nobel bequeathed little to his relatives, so they
    challenged the will in court and lost.

3. Nobel declared that his entire remaining estate
    should be used to endow "prizes to those who,
    during the preceding year, shall have conferred
    the greatest benefit to mankind." Not only was
    it highly unusual to donate large sums of money
    for scientific and charitable purposes at the time,
    Nobel essentially bequeathed his money to a
    non-existent foundation, which would have to be
    created posthumously.

4. Swedish leaders opposed dispersing the Swed-
    ish fortune to the rest of the world, stating it was
    immoral at a time when so many Swedes were
    impoverished.

5. Nobel's will named the groups to make the
    awards: the Karolinska Institute (medicine),
    the Swedish Academy of Sciences (chemistry
    and physics), the Swedish Academy (literature),
    and the Norwegian Parliament (peace). These
    institutions were responsible for the prize, yet

they held no qualifications for assuming such a responsibility.

6. That Nobel assigned the Peace Prize to the Norwegian Parliament aroused patriotic indignation in Sweden.

7. How could Nobel create a Peace Prize, when in fact he'd generated his vast fortunes by making explosives that could be used in war?

The Nobel Prize was the prize that almost didn't happen. By its very nature it was complex and multidimensional, and had numerous opponents. But it didn't die. Instead, it survived and flourishes to this day, now the most widely recognized and coveted group of prizes in the world.

Dynamite and Death

By all accounts, Alfred Nobel was a complex man—a scientist, an inventor, an entrepreneur, and an industrialist. But one has to wonder if his greatest and most overlooked strength was as a strategist. Throughout his life, he overcame a multitude of challenges, each with enormous odds. The most noteworthy being the taming of nitroglycerine into dynamite. But it was Nobel's last challenge, his will, that might have been his most difficult, for it was the one problem that he may have purposely decided not to solve himself.

One can only imagine what Nobel was contemplating as he wrote his will, but it's fair to assume he realized it would be controversial, challenged, and scrutinized by the world. After all, he had stipulated a vision that had never been created before, an international foundation. Second, it's conceivable that Nobel wanted his will to be as controversial as the inventions he profited from and the life he led. After all, in 1888 Alfred's brother Emil died in an explosion in one of Nobel's factories in Stockholm. The French newspapers incorrectly printed front-page obituaries noting Alfred as the deceased with the headlines, "The Merchant of Death is Dead." Third, Nobel's will was a challenge put forth to its executors (Ragnar Sohlman and Rudolf Lilljequist), his family, his country, and the world to do the right thing. In fact, Nobel once stated, "to spread knowledge is to spread well-being."

A fourth reason possibly helped shape Nobel's thinking at the time. The vision Alfred Nobel declared in his will was bigger and more complex than his ability to execute it. On the surface, this might seem uncharacteristic of a man who tamed nitroglycerin and built an industrial empire. However, Nobel had spent a lifetime dealing with the challenges and inner workings of various governments and legal systems around the world, so he knew how difficult and cumbersome they could be. For instance, in 1887 Nobel invented ballistite, a form of gunpowder that left behind no solid particles when it burned and was virtually smokeless. In the literature, it was described both as an "ingenious invention" and "the crowning glory" of Nobel. Nobel initially offered the patent to the French gunpowder monopoly, but they rejected it because they had developed their own product, Vieille powder. Nobel then offered it to Italy who accepted.

Since Nobel lived in France at the time, he was charged with industrial espionage and patent infringement, and threatened with imprisonment. The case was eventually dropped, but was behind his reason to leave France and move to Italy, where he bought a villa in San Remo and stayed until his death.

As Alfred Nobel penned his final will less than a year before his death, one must take into account the reflective soul that guided his words and his vision, for the vision he depicted was ingenious and the crowning glory of his life. But the genius didn't stop at the words he wrote. His true genius lay in how the vision became reality.

Create a Problem (CAP)

As Nobel was thoughtfully spelling out his wishes, it's fascinating to notice that he took a play out of his own playbook. In essence, Nobel focused on putting immense power into small, controllable packages. The vision spelled out in Nobel's will was the dynamite, and the will itself was the blasting cap. And when one reads and analyzes the historical papers surrounding the days following the reading of Alfred Nobel's will, this is exactly what happened. The pent-up energy from his family, the legal system, and local and foreign governments was immense. All he needed to do was create an explosive device made up of words and a vision, and then let it reach maximum pressure so rapidly that the shock wave shattered the norms.

> ALL HE NEEDED TO DO WAS CREATE AN EXPLOSIVE DEVICE MADE UP OF WORDS AND A VISION, AND THEN LET IT REACH MAXIMUM PRESSURE SO RAPIDLY THAT THE SHOCK WAVE SHATTERED THE NORMS.

There is no question that Nobel's solution was risky and could have easily failed. But in his heart, the Nobel Prize family had already become a reality when he inked his Last Will and Testament. With that vision, Nobel's life would transcend to a spiritual place that benefited mankind.

In effect, Alfred Nobel "Created A Problem" that he allowed the world to solve.

ELEVEN

The Whistleblower
Silent Problem Type—Ice Box

CONTENTIOUS ZONE

*First they ignore you. Then they laugh at you. Next
they fight you. Then you win.*

Mohandas K. Gandhi

In most stories, a major character is confronted with
a dilemma, often the challenge between "Doing what's
right" and "Doing the right thing." The tension between
these two is real and visible, and while the desired outcome is clear, the means to the outcome is sketchy and
treacherous at best. And the dilemma often feels bigger
than life itself. Such is the contentious landscape for the
whistleblower.

Whistleblower lawsuits emanate from silent problems, and upon occasion they embrace the CAP initiative philosophy. However, more often than not, they are unsuccessful. For instance, in 2008, a significant segment of the U.S. airlines industry came to a screeching halt when the Federal Aviation Administration (FAA) grounded hundreds of aircraft due to improper inspections and safety concerns as a result of two whistleblowers, Charalmabe "Bobby" Boutris and Douglas Peters, FAA inspectors. Bobby Boutris raised safety concerns regarding Southwest Airlines (SWA) via emails, memos, and meetings to his supervisor, Douglas Gawadzinski, and other FAA personnel, dating back to 2003. After repeated attempts by others to suppress his findings and silence his voice, Boutris sent a package to the Office of Special Council in August 2007. Following is a brief excerpt of Bobby Boutris's testimony to the Committee on Transportation and Infrastructure on March 30, 2008.

It is very sad that an FAA Safety inspector has to become a whistleblower in order to address safety issues... What you will find interesting is that in late March of 2007, after I discovered that SWA along with the FAA had allowed the operation of the aircraft with the overdue AD (Airworthiness Directives) inspections in revenue service and once everybody knew that I elevated this serious safety issue I was removed from my position and was placed under investigation due to an anonymous complaint with allegations against me....

In the end, Bobby Boutris was vindicated. However, he paid the price through professional exile, personal reprisal, and even a death threat. But the real challenge with any whistleblower action is that the discovery process tends to be long and arduous. During that process, the whistleblower is consistently and persistently exposed. For instance, Bobby Boutris said, "I am here to report that more than one FAA inspector along with FAA management have been looking the other way for years. No supervisor can do what my supervisor was doing without the support from fellow inspectors, the support of the Division Management Team (who were fully aware what was going on) and I believe with the support from some people in Washington." In essence, when a whistleblower exposes a problem, in reality they're often exposing a system, overrun with problems.

The Whistleblower CAP Initiative

In the end, most whistleblowers are marginalized. Some lose their homes, their families, and their communities. They become outcasts. Few become heroes for doing what's right. The Bobby Boutris story is different, and followed a similar trajectory to that of most CAP initiatives.

In the early stages of the problem, Bobby worked within the system, despite encountering many roadblocks. At each step of the journey, he was yelling, "Listen up everyone, we have a problem here. Why is it that I'm the only one who can see it?" In response, a game of "I'm the boss" and "You're an employee" unfolded.

For instance Boutris said, "I periodically met with Mr. Gawadzinski and voiced my concerns about the SWA AD compliance issues because I wanted to be proactive, not reactive. Mr. Gawadzinski told me again and again that he did not share my views and that he was the Principal and my Supervisor."

In the second phase, Boutris was marginalized. He noted, "I complained that since November 2006, when the Voluntary Disclosure Reporting Program had become web based for electronic submissions, I was the only Partial Program Manager in the office that did not have access because Mr. Gawadzinski had refused to give me a password."

In the third stage, Boutris was silenced. Gawadzinski told him, "He did not see a reason for me (Boutris) to stay in the office." In effect, Boutris was pushed out the door, hopefully never to be heard from again.

In the final act, Boutris created a CAP initiative by sending a packet to the Office of Special Council. And Bobby Boutris would be elevated to that of a hero.

CAP/WHISTLEBLOWER INITIATIVES ARE

HIGH-RISK SCENARIOS

The Bobby Boutris story is not atypical. CAP/Whistleblower initiatives are high-risk scenarios. It's no surprise the cards appear stacked against the whistleblower from the beginning. This is where patience and perseverance must be practiced, for the biggest challenge a whistleblower faces is gathering knowledge about their opponent, and this takes time. In essence, who is the problem important to? Who are the followers? What is their incentive to maintain the status quo? Once a whistleblower gets to the bottom of these issues, they better understand what/who they're up against and whether they should pursue the battle.

Around 400 BC, Sun Tzu wrote his classic treatise, *The Art of War*. Even today where warfare is commonly fought from a control room, it is still regarded as one of the greatest books on military strategy ever written. The tactics taught by Sun Tzu are explicit and profound, tactical and deliberate. The lessons possess as much relevance in the war room as in the creation of a CAP/whistleblower initiative. One of the basic tenants states that until you know the enemy, you cannot adequately prepare. Sun Tzu wrote:

1. He will win who knows when to fight and when not to fight.

2. He will win who knows how to handle both superior and inferior forces.

3. He will win whose army is animated by the same spirit throughout all its ranks.

4. He will win who, prepared himself, waits to take the enemy unprepared.

5. He will win who has military capacity and is not interfered with by the sovereign.

Although whistleblower provisions laid out by Sarbanes-Oxley simplify fact-finding dramatically for publicly traded companies, these tactics are relevant when deploying any CAP/whistleblower initiative. In most whistleblower situations, victorious whistleblowers innately:

- know when to fight

- come well prepared

- know who their opposition is.

Therefore, the first rule of every CAP/whistleblower initiative is to know thy enemy, who they are, what they smell like, and what they eat for breakfast, lunch, and dinner.

The second rule relates to data. In most scenarios, the whistleblower battlefield is won and lost with lots of hard, physical data. No he-said, she-said scenarios. The data has to be impeccable, able to withstand the scrutiny of the opposition and outside peer review. The data must be definitive in every aspect and contain numerous entries showing intent to deceive. This point is illustrated in Bobby Boutris's testimony when he stated, "I am here to report to you that all my findings and safety concerns have been validated 100%."

The third rule relates to values. A CAP/whistleblower initiative foundation is based on laws, processes, and procedures. Everything must be black and white.

The fourth, and possibly most important aspect, is tied back to leadership. In most instances, being a whistleblower is a lonely activity. It's a place where one can be his or her worst enemy. And a place where few errors in judgment or execution are tolerated. The whistleblower's character will be tested and his or her motives challenged. If one can pass this test, he or she has a chance for success.

In the end, Bobby Boutris and Douglas Peters did the right thing.

III

The Why,
the What,
and the How

TWELVE

Mental Maps and Inspiration

*To early explorers and geographers California repre-
sented a terrestrial paradise. It was Atlantis, Arcadia,
Avalon, El Dorado, the Garden of Eden, the Land of
Milk and Honey, the Pleasure Dome of Kublai Khan.*

Dora Polk, *The Island of California*

Myths and legends oftentimes have their roots in strange
and unexpected places, at times foretelling of distant
lands that contain great wealth and unexpected habi-
tants. Such is the literary origin of California. The 1510
novel by Garcia Ordonex de Montalvo, *Las Sergas de
Esplandi'an* describes a mythical place referred to as the
Island of California.

> *Know that on the right hand of the Indies there is
> an island called California very close to the side of
> the Terrestrial Paradise; and it is peopled by black*

women, without any man among them, for they live
in the manner of Amazons.

It told of a place that was rich in pearls and gold, and was a mere ten days journey from Mexico, and close to Asia and the East Indies.

Today, we know that California isn't an island after all, although it's one of the most progressive and richest states in North America. However, in the sixteenth century, seafaring explorers sought new lands that were believed to contain vast riches. Not surprisingly, explorers often searched for the mythical lands foretold in the legends of the time, even lands foretold in novels. For instance, the Spanish explorer Ponce de Le'on was in search of the Fountain of Youth when he traveled to present-day Florida in 1513. Although he never found the fabled spring, the legend lives on to this day. Likewise, Hernan Cortez, the famous Spanish explorer who conquered Mexico in 1521, was also influenced by such outside factors. The story goes that upon conquering Mexico, Cortez was in search of his next country to capture and conquer when he became captivated by the story told in Montalvo's novel. Cortez followed his passion by building ships on the western shores of New Spain (Mexico), and upon their completion, sent them north in search of the fabled Island of California.

The first of several expeditions set sail in 1533, discovering the Gulf of California and Baja, California. Subsequent expeditions pushed farther and farther north, reaching all the way up to the mouth of the Colorado River, the point that divides Mexico from the Baja

Peninsula. To Cortez's dismay, this proved the region was a peninsula, rather than an island as the novel had suggested.

Most stories would end here, where fiction faces the cross hairs of reality. California wasn't an island after all, and for close to a hundred years, maps showed California connected to the North American mainland. Then in 1622, a map by Michiel Colijn in Amsterdam depicted California as an island once again. This was followed up with a similar depiction in 1625 by Henry Briggs. This new illustration would become the default standard for maps for the remainder of the seventeenth century.

However, as the eighteenth century unfolded, fresh information from various explorers, including Jesuit missionary Father Eusbio Franciso Kino, raised critical concerns that California wasn't an island. For instance, Father Kino came to the conclusion that Baja was a peninsula, simply by walking from the mainland to the Baja coast. Yet despite this new information, mapmakers across much of Europe continued to propagate the error.

One can only imagine the numerous challenges mapmakers and explorers faced at the time. On one side of the fence was the long-standing belief that California was a large island, separated from the mainland. This belief was based on superstition and historical inaccuracies illustrating a point-of-view that had been perpetuated in various formats for several hundred years. On the other side of the equation was a new and emerging belief system, an idea based on old and new information. In this paradigm, California was thought to be part of the mainland and Baja as a peninsula.

Obviously, these widely divergent views were problematic, for maps by their very nature were highly treasured and thought to be accurate views of the world. But how does such a huge disparity that influences the worldview get started? How was the worldview propagated? And how does such a disparity get resolved?

In Dora Parks book, *The Island of California*, she writes:

> *California went on being represented as an island on innumerable maps throughout the seventeenth century. As a cartographic feature, it commanded wide attention. Yet in the same period, the real California receded once more into the shadows. The threats from foreign powers abated. There was no longer any urgency to crack "the northern mystery." Again the region was known only to passing galleons and the occasional pearl fisherman.*

In essence, the problem had grown silent. The sense of urgency to solve the problem had abated. Plus, the resources necessary to tackle the issue had all but dried up, so the inaccurate version was easy to accept and tolerate.

As is the situation with most CAP initiatives, someone possesses a passion to pursue a cause. In this instance, French mapmaker Guillaume de Lisle hadn't given up the fight. Instead, he challenged the existent belief system that accompanied the thinking at the time. For years, de Lisle poured through various records and documents, and at the end of his study he concluded that California wasn't an island. Then in 1722, de Lisle published a new map eliminating the "Island" depiction. Yet despite de Lisle's declaration, the effect of his new worldview would be mostly ignored, quite dissimilar to the effect of Colijn's map 100 years earlier. Therefore, the romantic and storied "Island of California" depiction would live on with mapmakers across much of Europe for several more decades.

Finally, twenty-five years after de Lisle's new worldview depiction, Ferdinand VII of Spain in 1747 issued a formal decree declaring that California was part of the mainland. The maps from that point forward would portray California in a new, more realistic light.

> A MENTAL MAP EXISTS INSIDE EVERY EMPLOYEE,
>
> EVERY ORGANIZATION, EVERY NATION, AND EVERY
>
> SOCIETY. THESE MAPS ARE BASED PARTIALLY UPON DATA,
>
> EXPERIENCE, PERCEPTION, INTUITION,
>
> AND EXISTENT WORLDVIEW.

Just as in the days of the Spanish explorers and cartographers, a mental map exists inside every employee, every organization, every nation, and every society. These maps are based partially upon data, experience, perception, intuition, and existent worldview. These information points are shaped into a mental map that becomes the basis from which everything else is filtered through and measured against. It becomes the basis for how things work, why things happen, and whether the system is aligned with the existent value statements, mission statements, and strategic plans.

As is often the case, we're prone to many of the same challenges that the mapmakers of the sixteenth and seventeenth centuries faced when trying to depict California. The world depicted isn't the world as it really is (i.e., this is the way things are supposed to work, yet this is how things really work). This is the underlying basis for the discovery of many silent problems. Take, for instance, the stories about Rosa Parks, Bobby Boutris, and Julie Gilbert. In each, the mental map believed in, and the map they had come to realize as true, were significantly different.

> THE UNDERLYING PREMISE FOR THEIR CAP INITIATIVE
>
> WAS TO BRING THE MAP BACK INTO ALIGNMENT
>
> WITH HOW THEY BELIEVED THE WORLD
>
> SHOULD REALLY WORK.

In each case, the underlying premise for their CAP initiative was to bring the map back into alignment with how they believed the world should really work, to initiate strategic and long-lasting change. Rosa Parks sat down and stayed seated. Bobby Boutris stood up and fought tirelessly for air safety. Julie Gilbert created WOLF. A CAP initiative is a high-performance change agent, a truth serum tool that can be calibrated and leveraged to tackle the really tough issues we face.

A CAP initiative approaches every silent problem from three angles:

1. We seek to make something we do not like go away.

2. We seek to make what we truly care about exist.

3. Silent problems must be transformed to make them act like a problem once again.

The first step is to lead with the solution because it's the most effective instrument for making what we truly care about exist. It's also an effective method to making a silent problem act like a problem again. However, to lead a CAP initiative from its infancy through to completion may require additional tools, levers, and competencies. What follows are four key areas that could be integral to a CAP initiative.

CHAPTER

THIRTEEN

Elements to Leverage in a CAP Initiative

Do one thing every day that scares you.

Eleanor Roosevelt

Imagine that you're Christopher Columbus in search of new trading routes to the West Indies. You're several months into the voyage, and you find that the winds are strong and the currents are swift. But then you suddenly enter an oceanic phenomenon called the Sargasso Sea—a place where there is no current, no wind, and no waves. When you initially cross the threshold to the Sargasso Sea, you're excited because it's filled with seaweed, which you consider a positive sign—land must be near. But when you try to determine the depth of the sea below the boat, you find no bottom. You conclude that there must be an abundance of fish here, yet you find very few. And then you become concerned that the seaweed is so thick it might entangle your boats, possibly hindering your journey.

The Sargasso Sea is an enigma, for the forces that make it so beautiful also defy logic. Located in the Atlantic Ocean between 20^0 to 35^0 North latitude and 30^0 to 70^0 West longitude, it is a 2-million-square-mile oval lens of water. It's a half-mile deep and rests in the colder reaches of the Atlantic Ocean. It lacks currents, yet is surrounded by some of the strongest currents in the world. Therefore, anything that drifts onto any of its surrounding currents eventually ends up in the Sargasso Sea.

As Columbus entered the Sargasso Sea, he could not explain the phenomenon. He could only stay the course, hoping to navigate a way out. Eventually the seas rose and he escaped its grasp. He entered the Gulf Stream and discovered a new world—North America.

Some CAP initiatives possess remarkable resemblance to Columbus's voyage and his encounter with the Sargasso Sea. In the early stages, everything is going according to plan; a swift victory is within reach. But then suddenly, the initiative gets sidetracked, pushed into the Sargasso Sea. But just like Columbus, one must be prepared to navigate the CAP initiative back on track, while at the same time keeping the initiative and its supporters energized. Four elements will help you navigate this part of the journey.

1. Make the Problem Visible and Memorable

People are obsessive about stupid things; they are persistent about important things.

William Ackman

As noted earlier, in a traditional problem-solving scenario, there tend to be five components leading the problem-solving process:

1. Identify the problem.

2. Gather data.

3. Analyze data.

4. Formulate a solution.

5. Implement the solution.

Remember, silent problems rarely respond to this linear approach. To openly define and engage others in a silent problem tends to be an effort in futility. In fact when you approach it from this angle, your most likely outcome will be a silent problem that remains silent. Instead, lead with a solution. When you lead with the solution, you create attention, the first step in making the problem visible. In Steve Denning's book, *The Secret Language of Leadership*, he succinctly asserts why this is so important:

Successful leaders communicate very differently from the traditional, abstract approach to communication. In all kinds of settings, they communicate by

following a hidden pattern; first they get attention.
Then they stimulate desire and only then do they
reinforce with reasons.
When the language of leadership is deployed in this
sequence, it can inspire enduring enthusiasm for a
cause and spark action to start implementing it.

> WHEN YOU LEAD WITH THE SOLUTION,
>
> YOU CREATE ATTENTION, THE FIRST STEP IN MAKING THE
>
> PROBLEM VISIBLE.

In a world where getting your message heard is so challenging, create a message that breaks through the noise barrier. Your CAP initiative must create and garner attention. To do this, make the message memorable. Here are three primary tactics to use:

1. **Create Top-of-Mind Awareness.** What's invisible often gets dismissed as unimportant. This is a significant challenge for a silent problem, and one you must avoid. When you create a top-of-mind awareness, you're less likely to be discounted. When Barbara launched her CAP initiative, she created a very tight and focused timeline—we will meet at 10:00 AM tomorrow morning in the conference room. Likewise, when Ragner Sohlman executed Alfred Nobel's will, Ragner knew that he was working against the clock. Being expedient and effective guided his every move and tactic.

2. **Create a Code Name.** When building on the top-of-mind theme, create a code name that resonates with the target audience. A code name implies a special meaning and purpose for the leaders, members, and supporters of the initiative. For instance, Julie Gilbert created WOLF. The name held special meaning and provided a passionate purpose for the CAP initiative.

3. **Create an Event.** At times, the best path to breaking through the noise barrier is to create an event that alters the way others see the world. When Rosa Parks stayed seated, she created an incident. When the black community boycotted the Montgomery bus system, they created an ongoing event that was highly memorable and challenged the worldview. When Bethune and Brenneman took the *Thou Shall Not* book out to the parking lot, their message was crystal clear. When a CAP initiative creates an event, it takes the problem out of the closet and places it on the front lawn for everyone to see.

2. Create a Sense of Urgency

We're on a mission from God.
from the movie *The Blues Brothers*

For many, the thought of creating a problem to solve a problem is illogical, even radical. It's definitely progressive. But when you face a problem that you're passionate about, all adjectives and concerns tend to get thrown out the window. In the movie *The Blues Brothers*, Jake (John Belushi) and his brother Elwood (Dan Aykroyd) take on a "mission from God" to save from foreclosure the Catholic orphanage where they were raised. To achieve their goal, they had to obtain $5,000 to pay the tax assessor by a specified date and time. They also had to become quite creative, avoiding Neo-Nazis, the police, and the military along the way. Jake and Elwood had a deeply rooted sense of urgency.

Without a doubt, a CAP initiative is a high-performance change-agent tool. Without Rosa Parks, I'm certain the civil rights movement would have been significantly altered. Without Alfred Nobel's insight, the industrial revolution would have been hampered and the possibility for the Nobel prizes never realized. Opportunity often seems cloaked in unusual places and associated with change.

But change is no easy initiative. Today, change is still the most challenging undertaking known to mankind, just as changing a map to represent reality was difficult to deploy in the seventeenth and eighteenth centuries. Harvard Business School professor and author John Kotter has written numerous books on change management, including his book *Leading Change*. He writes that creating an environment for change involves a multi-step process:

1. Get the urgency up.

2. Pull the right team together.

3. Communicate to the right people.

4. Empower others.

5. Create short-term successes.

6. Don't let the urgency subside.

Furthermore, Kotter says:

> *I've thought a lot about which of the steps people struggle with most. The answer, I believe is the first step: How to generate a real sense of urgency. A lot of people I talk to, unfortunately, don't understand how to do that very well... (source: S + B Online at a Glance, August 19, 2008)*

THE CAP INITIATIVE PROCESS THRIVES WHEN IT COMES

TO CREATING, BUILDING, AND SUSTAINING

A SENSE OF URGENCY.

I agree with Kotter that the "urgency factor" is too often overlooked, and one many leaders struggle to execute. My guess is that in some respects, we've lost our innate sense of urgency. Fortunately, the CAP initiative process thrives when it comes to creating, building, and sustaining a sense of urgency. For instance, Barbara sent out her email to her staff members after most had left for work and then followed it up with a meeting the following morning to discuss and implement. Julie Gilbert made the invitation to a select group of individuals with the instructions, "Just meet me...." A CAP initiative creates a sense of urgency because

1. A CAP initiative leads with the solution, not the problem—remember, people become attached to the solution.

2. A CAP initiative focuses on the desired outcomes, which are well defined, reasonable, and plausible.

3. A CAP initiative permits the tension inherent in the problem to be a positive factor in the process and a building block to achieving the desired outcome.

As I've studied and analyzed CAP initiatives, a sense of urgency is always important in achieving the desired outcome.

3. Allow Anger—Avoid Fear

You have nothing to fear, but fear itself.
Franklin D. Roosevelt

In the world of communications, the difference between anger and fear may appear miniscule, yet the distinction is immense. To a personnel manager, telling bad news is not for the weak at heart. Yet if done properly, it can empower and motivate; done poorly, it can humiliate and demean. To a marketing manager, sending a press release that informs competitors they have just been marginalized with a new product they're ready to introduce can paralyze the competitor's camp. If done poorly, the press release could merely anger them into action, and at a level not previously experienced. Likewise, in a CAP initiative, anger can motivate individuals and team to take action, making it happen. Fear could simply keep them quiet, enabling the silent problem to continue its somber sleep.

In recent years, numerous scientific studies have quantified these distinctions. In essence, fear tends to lead people to more pessimistic judgments about risk in future events, whereas anger leads to more optimistic judgments. For example, the business scandals promulgated by the likes of Worldcom, Tyco International, Enron, and others could result in multiple outcomes. If the government allowed fear to take hold, like during the depression era of the 1930s, people would simply hoard their money under mattresses and in tin cans in the backyard. The economy and trust in the stock market would suffer. Or the government could enable its citizens to become angry, thereby securing a different future. Anger could become the impetus to implement quick regulatory changes, making the public more optimistic about the probability of a successful change in the system and, ultimately, a more positive future.

If you are to change the tone, the key in crafting your message lies in defining the desired outcome. Leaders like Winston Churchill, Abraham Lincoln, and others have capitalized on the power of anger to move communities and nations forward. Despite the bad situations, they realized that channeling one's anger can create positive

WITHOUT WARNING

and long-term results. Martin Luther King Jr. once said, "The supreme task is to organize and unite people so that their anger becomes a transforming force."

> MARTIN LUTHER KING JR. ONCE SAID, "THE SUPREME TASK IS TO ORGANIZE AND UNITE PEOPLE SO THAT THEIR ANGER BECOMES A TRANSFORMING FORCE."

At the opposite end of the barometer lies fear. Because fear helps us avoid things like pain and death, it serves an essential role in the survival process. However, fear in the CAP initiative framework can be devastating. Teams that once worked together might suddenly disintegrate. Your vision is replaced with a lack of vision. Personal significance is replaced with personal insignificance. Individuals fight to survive, ultimately leaving the initiative behind. Fear, in many instances, creates paralysis.

The distinction between the two commonly lies in the message. Anger needs a third person, a "whipping boy" so to speak. Winston Churchill needed Hitler to rally a nation. Martin Luther King Jr. needed the injustice shown toward blacks to heighten his cause to national status. Such is the power of anger if focused and channeled properly.

There's a saying, "When the going gets tough, the tough get going." Strong CAP initiatives channel their messages in a way to avoid fear, and instill anger. Anger instills a sense of hope and an opportunity for a bright future. Maybe the saying should be, "When the going gets tough, the tough get angry!"

4. The Power of Influence

Those who influenced their world had a fire within,
an almost magical alignment between being,
actions and words. Unfocused photons merge into an
energized laser beam. The authentic leader embodies
his or her vision, and expresses inner congruence
through a million verbal and non-verbal cues that
everyone in the organization observes.

Gene C. Mage, syndicated columnist

The goal of every CAP initiative is to influence. It's that simple and that complex. If the initiative succeeds, the silent problem must become visible, it must be acknowledged and a solution implemented. To achieve this outcome, the CAP initiative must influence the target audience. In fact, the ability to influence is often regarded as the single most important quality a leader could possess. It's at the very heart and soul of leadership, and without it, leaders would be unable to lead. It is the enabler of change and an essential building block of human civilization.

In the context of a CAP initiative, Dr. Robert Cialdini, author of *Influence: The Psychology of Persuasion*, notes that influence occurs at the point when a person arrives at a set of circumstances, encounters a particular principle, or says "that's enough; I feel secure in my decision, and it's okay to move forward." At that point, influence has been achieved. Therefore, the need to influence is an integral component of every CAP initiative. Dr. Cialdini identifies these six traits linked to influence:

- **Scarcity.** People need to know what benefits they'll gain, and lose if they don't choose your direction.

- **Liking.** People need to identify with positive connections like similarities, compliments, or cooperative endeavors. What's important, though, is not whether your follower likes you, but rather, whether your follower believes that you like them.

- **Social Proof.** People instinctively look to others like themselves for confirmation. Testimonials commonly create social proof, and in many instances, rumors kill social proof.

- **Reciprocation.** If I give you something, you probably feel obliged to reciprocate the favor. It's the old give-and-take philosophy.

- **Authority.** When a person recognizes your expertise, the barriers begin to erode. The unspoken message of titles, offices, and experiences help you develop a status of personal or organizational authority. A second aspect of authority is being trustworthy.

- **Commitment and Consistency.** People want to be consistent with what they have said, done, and committed to in the past. Once you commit to something, you want to appear consistent with that commitment. Personal commitment is highly valued by society.

Influence is an important element of the CAP initiative model. With influence, you have a position of commitment, rather than compliance. The initiative catalyzes an organization's collective soul through words, actions, and presence. It's able to instill and propagate a unique DNA code, an *esprit de corps*, a collective mind. It understands the invisible, and doesn't fear it. And in the end, the CAP initiative influences the outcome.

> WITH INFLUENCE, YOU HAVE A POSITION OF COMMITMENT, RATHER THAN COMPLIANCE.

FOURTEEN

Pulling It All Together

You need to be fighting for that idea as opposed to just having it accepted. That process of being misunderstood helps you figure out how to communicate it in a way that other people can hear.

Brad Anderson, CEO, Best Buy

The famous architect Buckminster Fuller designed the geodesic dome, and actually adopted its principles as a way of life. Fuller in 1928 writes, "These new homes are structured after the natural system of humans and trees with a central stem or backbone, from which all else is independently hung, utilizing gravity instead of opposing it. This results in a construction similar to an airplane, light, taut, and profoundly strong."

When one looks at the elements of a CAP initiative and how they're woven together, it possesses a structure similar to Buckminster Fuller's geodesic dome. As you build your CAP initiative, you'll find yourself moving through four phases, similar to Fuller's geodesic design:

The Genesis Phase. The first step for a CAP initiative is to identify and acknowledge that a problem exists, i.e., the central backbone. Not surprisingly, this tends to be an inside-out game, for it's the individuals who are closest to the problem who can see it for what it's worth. At times, this might be an employee or an associate whose job is being affected in a negative way. At other times, it could even be a client, customer, or friend who has experienced a problem, yet are concerned it isn't being resolved to their satisfaction.

> IT'S THE INDIVIDUALS WHO ARE CLOSEST TO THE PROBLEM WHO CAN SEE IT FOR WHAT IT'S WORTH.

Under most situations, the individuals who have been exposed to the problem directly or indirectly are likely the same individuals with the passion to solve it. In the early stages, a slight curiosity might take hold. Yet over time, they become infatuated with the problem and the many challenges it possesses, eventually working forward toward a solution. Along that journey, a multitude of questions should be asked and answered. Some of these might include the following:

1. To the best of my knowledge, does a problem truly exist?

2. If a problem exists, is it important? And to whom?

3. To the best of my knowledge, is the problem truly silent? And why do I believe this is the case?

4. If it is silent, why is it silent? Lack of knowing? Neglect? Corruption? Habit?

5. If a silent problem is present, is it really worth solving? Why?

6. If it's worth solving, who is going to make it happen?

The answers to these and other questions become the backbone from which everything else is hung. It's the basis for moving forward, or not.

The Incubation Phase. Every CAP initiative tends to move through an incubation phase where questions are asked, ideas are challenged, and solutions explored. During this phase, you must complete three activities:

1. **Acknowledge a leader for the CAP initiative.** The role of the leader is to create a clear vision, build the trust and respect of others, and pull together a group of individuals (optional) focused toward a single cause. The leader becomes the heart, the soul, and the passion for the initiative.

2. **Develop a solution to the silent problem.** The solution should be simple to understand and easily implemented. The solution could include relative information such as price, ROI, or time.

3. **Identify the entry point for the solution.** A CAP initiative must identify an entry point where it can be heard and positively acted upon. To find this, ask these questions:

- What is the silent problem's origin?

- Can the origin be attached to a person or a group?

- Could someone have a vested interest in keeping it silent?

- Are there any economic consequences to the problem?

- Have previous attempts to solve the problem occurred? If yes, what were the circumstances, what challenges did the project face and what was the outcome?

These questions identify where the silent problem resides. Once you answer the questions, launch your CAP initiative one to two levels higher in the hierarchy of the organization. If one shoots too low in the organizational ladder, a Chicken Little scenario could easily unfold, greatly hindering the initiative. Instead, the CAP initiative should be placed where it can be heard, appreciated, and positively acted upon.

> IF ONE SHOOTS TOO LOW IN THE ORGANIZATIONAL LADDER, A CHICKEN LITTLE SCENARIO COULD EASILY UNFOLD, GREATLY HINDERING THE INITIATIVE.

The Response Phase. Now that an entry point has been identified, the next step is to lead with the solution, making the problem visible. Remember:

People identify with the problem; they become attached to the solution.

When you launch a solution, you'll begin to learn an individual's true convictions and sentiment regarding the problem. It is the ultimate truth serum. And we mustn't forget. The solution defines the problem.

If the CAP recipient identifies, accepts, and becomes aligned with the solution, then it's just a matter of time before you execute the solution. However, if the recipient disagrees with the solution or denies that a problem even exists, it is time to reinforce the solution. How? By releasing more information, usually in the areas surrounding the following:

- **Money.** Not surprisingly, money tends to be an integral component inside most problems. Those who lack or lose control of money are inevitably weakened. Whoever controls or can directly influence money has a powerful position to make things happen. The individual who can leverage the money component in their favor gains critical momentum.

MONEY TENDS TO BE AN INTEGRAL COMPONENT INSIDE

MOST PROBLEMS.

- **Data.** Disclosing data that supports the CAP initiative can be a strong determinant in getting noticed and the road toward success. When data is strong, the recipient of the CAP initiative is more likely to take you seriously and will become more likely to negotiate in good faith. Data becomes the truth serum that no one can run away from.

> DATA BECOMES THE TRUTH SERUM THAT NO ONE CAN
>
> RUN AWAY FROM.

- **Values.** How do the values of the CAP initiative align with the stated values of the recipient or the organization? Help the recipient realign his or her mental map with the reality of what's happening and why it's important.

At this juncture, most recipients of a CAP initiative will at least agree that a problem exists, although they might disagree on the solution presented. When this occurs, you're in the BOILS Zone. The leaders of the CAP initiative should negotiate with the opposing party to formulate an altered solution. For some, this may look like compromise; for others, this is victory. The question is, what are the leaders of the CAP initiative and their followers willing to accept as a new solution?

The Challenge Phase. If the recipient of the CAP initiative doesn't acknowledge that a problem exists or is unwilling to negotiate, your next step increases in complexity, for this is the Contentious Zone. It's at this point that you realize this could be a long, drawn out process. But even here, there are tactics you can use. Once again, reinforce with the money, data, and values trifecta, kicking it up a notch or two. Show the CAP recipient that you're well prepared and ready for the next step, if this is where they want to take it.

In addition to money, data, and values, you have one trump card you can play. Escalate the problem. Often, this is the point where you realize that you've launched the CAP initiative too low in the organizational hierarchy. If this occurs, be prepared to escalate it a minimum of one to two levels higher in the organization, possibly all the way up to the Board of Directors and, upon rare occasion, to the news media or into the judicial system.

As you proceed through the CAP initiative process, you'll identify specific juncture points. Or as Sun Tzu noted, "Water shapes its course according to the nature of the ground over which it flows." And it's at these points where you must proceed according to plan, increase the velocity of the initiative, or concede defeat. Remember, everything starts if and when the recipient agrees that a problem exists.

FIFTEEN

Beyond Ideas

*You don't just deal with adversity—you use it
to propel you forward.*
Erick Weihenmayer, first blind person to summit
Mt. Everest

In Book VII of the Republic, Greek philosopher Plato
tells the story of, "The Allegory of the Cave." A group
of men were held prisoner in a cave, their necks and feet
bound so all they could do was look at the wall in front
of them, with a fire behind that projected shadows on
the wall. Over time, the shadows they could see and the
noises they could hear became their perception of reality. Then one day, one of the prisoners breaks loose and
discovers that the images emanated from a stage where
puppet-handlers held up various objects found in the real
world. What the men believed was real were only shadows on the wall.

Today, do our organizations operate from a perspective of shadows on the wall? Is our understanding of the real world comparable to the puppet-handlers on a stage? I suggest we need to know! For starters, we must recognize that silent problems occur right here in broad daylight, where we work, live, and play. They're real, and we ought to start thinking about them and contemplating how they affect each of us. If we leave them to their own device, their sting could be profound.

We must encourage and empower those around us who might unearth and identify the silent problems. Although they might be frightened about what could happen, they must be assured that they are safe and their solutions honored. If they come forward, they'll tell the world what they're really passionate about. In the case of Julie Gilbert, it was about the women inside Best Buy and how they could become a valued constituent of the management team and the organization as a whole. For Alfred Nobel, it was about a higher cause and purpose. For Bobby Boutris, it was about safety of the airline industry. In each of these instances, these leaders visualized the world differently. And along the way, they instilled and propagated a single-minded focus. They understood the invisible and didn't fear it. They were willing to tackle the really tough problems and, in the end, change the world.

Peter Drucker once said, "The best way to predict the future is to create it." Create your future by building a culture where silent problems are not ignored. Some of the most challenging problems our organizations and society will face in the twenty-first century will be silent problems. Our greatest threat does not come from outside in the form of competitors or new world players, but from within. The saying, "I've seen the enemy and it is I," holds true. Arm your organization for a better future today. Prepare employees for the silent problems they might face or encounter, and show them how to deal with them. These employees may become your competitive advantage in our increasingly complex and competitive world.

Lastly, be committed to educating your organization about silent problems and what to do about them.

Perhaps Plato held the key insight into silent problems when he said, "May they have the wisdom to know the difference between light and knowledge." I encourage you to shine light on the silent problems in your organization.